A Treasury of

Quilt Labels

Susan McKelvey

©1993 by Susan Richardson McKelvey

All photographs by Celia Pearson, Annapolis, Maryland

Illustrations by Susan Senesi, Annapolis, Maryland

Cover designs by Dawnell Reeves, adapted and made by Susan McKelvey, and photographed by Celia Pearson. Cover calligraphy by Kathleen Balamuth, Artability, Orinda, California

Editing by Louise Owens Townsend

Technical editing by Joyce E. Lytle

Design and production coordination by Gillian Johnson, Merrifield Graphics, Hanover, Maryland

Published by C & T Publishing, P. O. Box 1456, Lafayette, California 94549

ISBN 0-914881-55-8

Library of Congress Cataloging-in-Publication Data

McKelvey, Susan Richardson.
   A treasury of quilt labels / by Susan McKelvey.
   p. cm.
   Includes bibliographical references.
   ISBN 0-914881-60-4
   1.Quilting. 2. Labels—Design I. Title.
TT835.M47   1993
746.9'7—dc20
                        92-46212

Calligraphic Permanent Pen, Callipen, Fashion Craft Fabric Markers, Identi-pen, and Pigma Micron are
   trademarks of Sakura Color Products Corporation of America
Glory is a registered trademark of EdMar Company
See-Thru is a trademark of Pelle's
Stencil Magic Paint Creme is a registered trademark of Delta Technical Coatings, Inc.
Y&C Fabricmate and Y&C Permawriter II are trademarks of Yasutomo and Company

Printed in the United States
First Edition

9   8   7   6   5   4   3   2   1

Contents

Part One: The Background

Part Two: The Techniques

Part Three: The Labels

Part Four: Tying Up Loose Ends

To Doug, Leslie and Scott McKelvey

Chance cannot change my love, nor time impair.

Robert Browning

Acknowledgments

Many hands make light work.

Old English Proverb, 1460

Many hands have truly made the work of *A Treasury of Quilt Labels* not only lighter but richer and more exciting! It is with a humble heart that I thank the designers for their contributions: Pele Fleming, Sandy Flores, Jackie Janovsky, Anna Macaluso, Rhoda Miller, Dawnell Reeves, Nancy Tribolet, and Pauline Trout. These talented artists, each focusing on her specialty, have given us inspiration for our own exploration of quilt labels.

My heartfelt thanks go to my editor, Louise Townsend, for tactful and humorous guidance in keeping me on schedule and within word count; my artist, Susan Senesi, whose delicate artwork beautifully depicts the flavor of 19th-century inkings; and to Gillian Johnson, my designer and friend, for molding my vision into the gift I wanted to give to my fellow quilters.

Thanks, too, to Diane Pedersen, whose faith in me has seen us through many delightful times together, and to the beloved folks at C & T, who make writing and publishing a joy!

Susan McKelvey

December 1992
Millersville, Maryland

4

Part One

The

Background

Lest Our Labors be Forgotten and Our Heritage Lost

I have admired, cherished, and pondered over the quilts made by our forebears. So few of these quilts were signed. Were the makers too modest to attach their names to their work? Did they think that the work wasn't significant? That the maker wasn't important? That the quilts would not last so long that unknown generations would look at them? How sad. Even with the few quilts that were signed, there is precious little information about the maker or makers, usually just a name, and possibly the date.

The work ***was*** significant, the makers ***were*** important, and the quilts ***did*** last—at least enough of them to whet our appetite for information and to inspire an entire quilt renaissance. And we, that unknown future generation, are searching for the answers to many questions about the makers of the quilts made over a century ago.

Just as the women of the 19th century did not foresee a need to document the making of their quilts, I fear there are too many of us today who cannot believe that the quilts we are making are important to more than just our loved ones. We are not signing them, and worse, we are not documenting them.

Our quilts are part of the history of women. They are part of the quilt revival of the late 20th century. They are greater than ourselves and, as such, deserve to be documented.

We owe it to our descendants to tell them about our part in this historic revival. We owe them, at the very least, the names, dates, and places involved in the making of our quilts.

Thus, labels. A label is an easy and logical way to provide documentation information on a quilt. Because it rests on the back of the quilt, it doesn't interfere with the design. It needn't be thought about until after the quilt is finished, and it is as simple to add as the binding. The information you provide is essential as a record of the creative process. You can, of course, work any of the information into the quilt top, but if you don't want to do that, add a label.

Is it worth the time to make a fancy label? I say, "Yes!" The label, just as much as the binding and the backing, is a finishing touch. A label makes a profound statement.

Let our generation of quilters say more than, "When this you see, Remember me." Let us say instead:

"When this you read, Know me, indeed."

It is a sad fact of life today that quilts are being stolen at an increasing rate. As people begin to realize that quilts are valuable, these treasured items have become worth stealing. Make your quilt less desirable to a thief by making it impossible to get rid of the documentation on the quilt! One way is to quilt the label right into the quilt, so it must be cut out, not just snipped off. Force thieves to deface your quilt and decrease its value if they want to hide its origins.

Sewing the label onto the backing before quilting and quilting it along with the quilt can accomplish this. It requires a little more careful planning when you're sandwiching the quilt top and backing, but it is worth it. It also requires that you make the label before you begin quilting, but this, too, is worth it.

Plan where you want the label to be on the quilt back. The simplest place is a lower corner, but any place is fine. Just as you plan how wide an overlap to leave on the backing, plan your label to be inside this at least 6" and appliqué it onto the backing, keeping it straight. Trim away the backing behind the label so you won't have an extra layer through which to quilt. When you sandwich the quilt top and backing, take extra care to be sure the corner containing the label is straight and well-basted. Then forget it and quilt. I have found that whatever design I quilt on the front looks fine on the label. The quilting doesn't have to be specifically planned for the label. Quilting the label into the quilt makes that label an integral part of the quilt.

Documentation
To Include on Labels

What should be on a label? This is up to you—it is a personal choice that changes with each quilt and each label. Definitely, we should include the basics: Who? What? When? Where? Why? and How?

Who?	Who is it for? Who made it?
What?	What type of quilt is it? What is its name? What inspired the design?
When?	When was it made?
Where?	Where was it made?
Why?	Why was it made? A wedding? An anniversary? A graduation? A birthday? A goodbye?
How?	How was it made? How is it appropriate for the recipient?

In addition to the basics, you might want to include a message, a poem, or a quotation.

I see these labels as sentimental records first, not identification labels. So I see, for example, that the "Where?" question on the label might contain the town and state but not necessarily the address and phone number. But for the recipient, include full names. "To Bert and Betty" could refer to Albert or Egbert or Bertrand. Instead, write, "To Albert and Elizabeth Primrose." For documentation purposes, a last name is necessary. Ask any of the quilt historians doing research today about how they have traced the quiltmakers of bygone eras. The minimum information needed includes the full names, town, state, and date. From that information, researchers can find records about families in an area. At a minimum, I would like the family members of future generations to be able to say with authority whether Great Grandma Helen in 1992 or Great Aunt Susan in 1998 made the quilt they know was made sometime in the 1990s.

Phrases To Use on Labels

To whom is the quilt being given?   *To Albert and Elizabeth Primrose*

Why?   *for their 50th Anniversary*
on the occasion of their 50th Anniversary
on their 50th Anniversary

Who made the quilt?   *Made by Sandra Dulles*
Made with Love by Sandra Dulles
Made with Affection by Sandra Dulles
Made by their daughter, Sandra Dulles

Where and when was the quilt made?   *Freesoil, Michigan*
January 1993

Made in Freesoil, Michigan
January 1993

Made at Oak Knoll Cottage
Freesoil, Michigan
January 1993

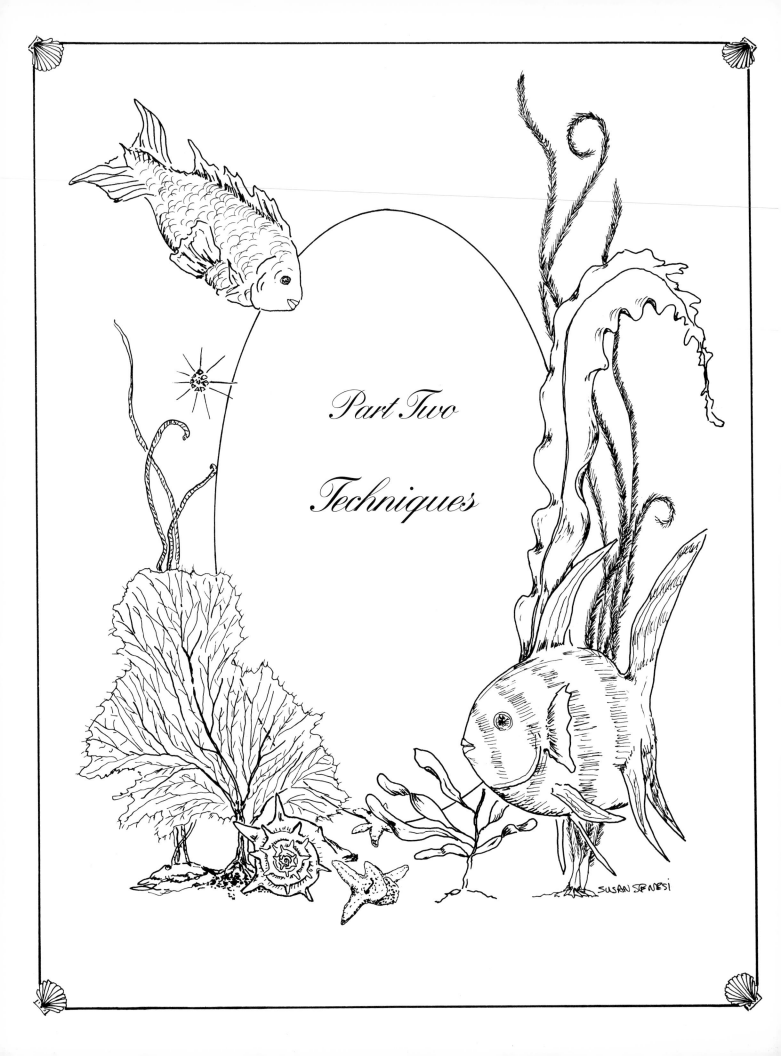

Part Two

Techniques

SUSAN SENESI

Chapter 1
Designing Your Labels

SIZE

A label may be any size. There is no "correct" size. This said, there are several useful considerations:

1. **Size should be proportionate to the quilt.** A tiny wall hanging respectfully requests a tiny label. A full-sized quilt can handle a larger label.

2. **Size should be proportionate to what will be written on it.** A label for a group quilt with lots of information should be large. If your handwriting is large, you need more space. If you have lots to say—a poem or a long message—design a large label.

3. **Size should be proportionate to the decoration.** If you really want to put a particular element on the label—say, an appliquéd flower from the front—and it is quite large (or easier to appliqué full size), make your label large enough to accommodate that element.

4. **Size should be able to accommodate the pen used.** A thick-pointed pen that makes heavy lines needs to be used on a large space. Conversely, a tiny, fine-line inking might be lost on a large label.

SHAPE

1. **Edges should be easy to appliqué.** That is why I tend to design so the outside edges are straight or at least simple in shape. They then provide an easy turning line to appliqué.

2. **Echo the front.** A label may be any shape. There is no reason to make a label rectangular or square. Consider what I call the "echo" theory here. Try echoing on the back some element from the front. This ties the two together. If you have fans on the quilt top, why not a fan-shaped label? If stars, repeat the stars. Look for an element on the front that either has enough space on it for writing or in which the space could be adapted for writing.

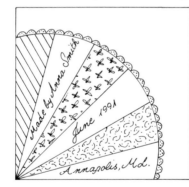
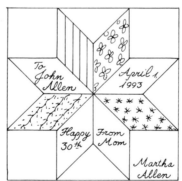

3. **Use a block from the front.** Most blocks can be adapted for signing simply by substituting light-colored fabric for whatever color you used in the block. Look at the blocks in your quilt to see how one could be used as a label.

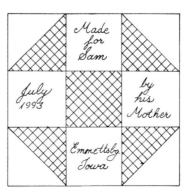

4. **Use a shape from the front.** You needn't use an entire block. Perhaps choose a pretty shape (for example, a diamond) from the quilt top. Use the proportions, but enlarge the shape as needed. Or choose any appliqué element. Use a favorite flower, heart, or basket and appliqué it in the corner of your label.

5. **Use an element from a fabric on the front.** Look at the large prints on the quilt front for shapes that might be cut out and appliquéd onto the label. Flowers, animals, appealing shapes—any of these can embellish the label and tie it to the quilt front. *Leslie's Graduation* on page 33 and *Quick Strawberries* on page 34 are examples of this method. Elements were cut out and appliquéd onto the backgrounds to make labels that echo the front of the quilt.

DESIGN

1. **Design includes both the writing and the decoration.** Once you have chosen the size of your label, draw the outline on graph paper and make five to ten copies to play with. Sometimes it helps to cut out the paper to the actual size. This is useful for visualizing the perimeters of the label.

2. **List the information you want to include to get a feeling for how much space you need.** Are you going to include only some of the basics (who? what? when? where? why? and how?) or are you going to include a verse or message? Try writing the information on the paper labels several times in different positions to see how it might look and how much space it might fill.

3. **Consider spacing.** The most important information on the label is the documentation information. The decoration is secondary. Plan enough space in the center area to write the information you want to include in the size label you want to use.

4. **Consider where to focus the design.**

Four corners

A very stable and clean design because it is balanced.

Two corners

Choose top left and bottom right because we read from top to bottom and left to right. To achieve balance, either make the two designs equal or put the larger design in the top left corner and the smaller one in the bottom right corner.

One side

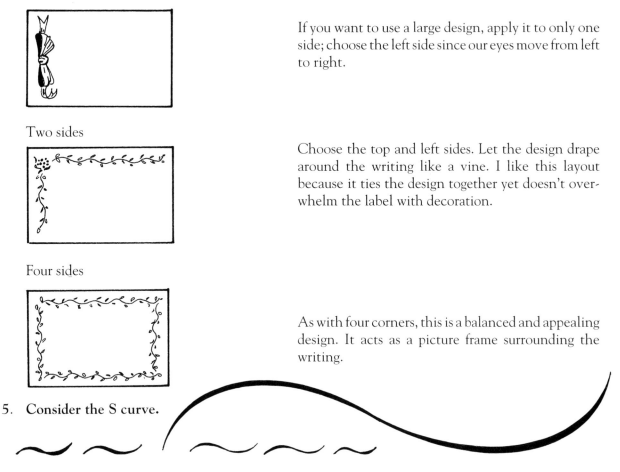

If you want to use a large design, apply it to only one side; choose the left side since our eyes move from left to right.

Two sides

Choose the top and left sides. Let the design drape around the writing like a vine. I like this layout because it ties the design together yet doesn't overwhelm the label with decoration.

Four sides

As with four corners, this is a balanced and appealing design. It acts as a picture frame surrounding the writing.

5. **Consider the S curve.**

When laying out any design, keep the S curve in mind. It is the loveliest of lines. Whether you are incorporating ribbon, appliqué, *broderie perse*, drawing, or any other decorative method, try to use the S curve within your layout. There are times when you want a clean, straight line. There are others when you want to soften the design with a curve. The S curve is always appealing.

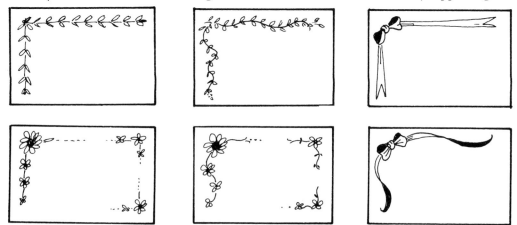

6. **Lay out the label.** Draw or actually lay out the full-size pattern pieces for any design elements. Draw a sketch on paper or lay out the actual elements on the background fabric. Only when you are satisfied with the layout should you pin and sew. If you are using a design from this book, trace the elements in pencil, then adapt them in size, if necessary. Each technique requires specific methods, which are included in each section.

Chapter 2
Permanent Pens

The pen you use on your label is of major importance because you want the information to be readable for a long time to come.

Only you can determine which pen is best for your quilt. Remember that when writing on fabric you will want ease of writing, permanence, and non-bleeding ink. Only a few pens on the market fulfill all of these requirements.

There are several pens that I feel comfortable recommending. None is without flaws, and all should be tested on *your* fabric and with the probable washing circumstances of your quilt in mind. A child's quilt may be washed hundreds of times. A presentation quilt may rarely be washed. And remember, if your quilt is a gift, you will give up control of how it is cared for. Will the owners cherish it as you would? Probably not. Will their dogs sleep on it? Will their children bounce on it? Will their cat throw up on it? Or shred it with feline claws? Will it be washed often? Your gift of love may be loved in ways different from those you intended. Fabric may fade; the label may, too. Do your best, give with love, and let the quilt pass on to its destiny.

I have experimented with the following pens and have found these characteristics:

Sakura Pigma Micron™

This is a wonderful pen for writing on fabric. It comes in various colors and in several point sizes. The lower the number on the pen, the finer the point (the points range from .005 through .08). All colors are not available in all point sizes. The ink is waterproof, acid-free, and doesn't bleed. I use the .01 pen for most of my writing because it produces a fine but visible line. Because the point is so fine, the trick to using the Pigma pen on fabric is to write slowly (taking the time to form the letters) and with a light touch so the pen doesn't drag.

Sakura Identi-pen™

The Identi-pen is a two-pointed permanent pen designed for marking on many surfaces from fabric to vinyl. It comes in several colors. The ink flows a bit faster than that of the Pigma so you need to write a little faster. The ink doesn't bleed much as you write, and the two points provide variety in lettering size. Both points are much thicker than those of the Pigma Micron but have sharp tips that insure precise lines. I use the Identi-pen when I want large or dark writing.

Sakura Callipen™ Calligraphy Pen

The Callipen is a chisel-pointed calligraphy pen that contains the same pigment ink as the Pigma and, thus, is permanent on fabric. It comes in six colors (black, red, blue, green, brown, and rose). The ink flow is light so sometimes you need to go over a letter to achieve good resolution, but there is no bleeding, and the color variety is welcome.

Sanford Calligraphic Permanent Pen™

This calligraphy pen has permanent ink and comes in two point sizes (1.5mm and 2.5mm) and only one color (black). It washes well under test circumstances, and the ink flow is excellent on the first stroke, providing a dark, clear line. However, your lettering must be quite large to accommodate the pen's point, so it is useful for larger writing projects.

Y & C Fabricmate™

These pens come in two point sizes and many colors. Because they are designed for use on fabric, they wash well. The ink flow is not thick; sometimes you have to go over a letter twice. As with the Sanford

Calligraphy pen, the letters turn out quite large. But those who want to do calligraphy on fabric will welcome the opportunity to experiment.

Y & C PermaWriter II™

The PermaWriter writes well on fabric. The ink flow is faster than that of the Pigma, and some people find this an advantage. The pen bleeds more than the Pigma, so you can—and must—write faster on the fabric. This makes it a good pen for inexperienced writers who want to write on fabric as they would on paper. The brown is a lovely chocolate brown and complements the rust brown of the Pigma, so I use both pens, frequently in combination.

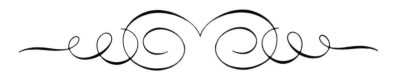

TEST ALL PENS

Always test any pen you want to use with the particular fabric you are considering. Pens react differently to different fabrics. Some things will help, though:

1. Writing on 100%-cotton fabric works best. The more polyester there is in a fabric, the more bleeding will occur.

2. Prewash your fabric. This is to remove all sizing, which can act as a barrier to ink penetration.

3. Test the pen with your particular fabric. Write on several different pieces. You will find that one pen writes beautifully on one fabric and grabs on another. Or it bleeds on one and not on another. You want to know these characteristics **before** you write on your beautiful label. If you like the point of one particular pen but it bleeds on your fabric, try changing fabrics.

4. Wait 24 to 48 hours before test washing. Some people find that this helps the ink to "set." If the pen's instructions tell you to set another way, do so. Some pen manufacturers recommend heat setting, or at the very least, they say, "It can't hurt."

5. Wash the test scraps in different wash situations. For example, if a quilt is washed the way it should be washed, it will be soaked in a tub for only four minutes in cold water and with a very delicate detergent. Wash one scrap this way. Give another scrap the full detergent treatment, and see what happens. Too often, in a test situation, one throws the test scrap into a normal, heavy wash with bleach and then wonders why the ink fades. Try several settings: cold, warm, etc. This should give you a good idea of how your pen and fabric wash together.

Chapter 3
Embellishing Your Handwriting

In order to make beautiful labels, you must be able to write beautifully on fabric. This requires learning some techniques and doing a bit of practicing. The exciting thing is that we all can embellish our handwriting, using just a few well-chosen techniques. Once you have mastered them, you, too, will be a master of writing on quilts.

You don't have to learn Spencerian hand or calligraphy in order to embellish your handwriting. A few well-chosen swoops, flourishes, tails, and sweeping S curves will contribute to a look of elegance.

Practice each technique on fabric. Use a good-quality, 100%-cotton muslin, prewashed and ironed. Use a Pigma .01 pen for your first efforts. Later, you can switch to any size that is appropriate to your writing project. Remember, with a Pigma .01, write slowly and lightly or the pen will drag.

1. **Add curves and tails to the beginning and ending letters in words.** The S curve is attractive added to anything in any size.

    Not This   *Thelma*   But This   *Thelma*

    Lois   *Lois*

2. **Extend the ends of uppercase letters or of the last letter in a word way under the word.**

    Love ~ Merry ~ Helen ~ Sincerely

3. **Don't worry about the slant of your writing.** Although 19th-century script had a pronounced right slant, the the embellishment techniques work on backhand just as well. Keep the slant that is most comfortable for you and add swoops and flourishes as you please.

    Hope ~ Family ~ friendship

4. **Add contrast.** Go over one side of each letter again with the pen. This gives the look of calligraphy and makes the letters more elegant. It doesn't seem to matter which side of a letter you go over or that you always choose the same side. It's the illusion of dark and light that counts.

    Add Contrast ~ Add Contrast

5. **Think about proportion.** In 19th-century script, the relative proportion between upper and lowercase letters was much greater than in our script today. Try making the uppercase letters and loop letters much larger than the lowercase letters. This gives the spidery look of 19th-century hand.

    Friendship ~ Hope

Enjoy embellishing your writing, but remember to keep your signature recognizable when you are actually signing your work. Someday, someone may want to compare that signature to your letters and documents. Help them!

Chapter 4
Planning and Spacing Your Words

1. **Decide what information you want to include.**
   To Leslie M. McKelvey
   Upon her graduation from the University of Michigan, May 1992
   Signed by her Sisters of A Δπ
   With love from Mom
   Millersville, Maryland, 1991-1992

2. **Decide how you want to phrase the information and in what order. Write it out.**

3. **Decide the size of your label inside the decorative border or decoration**—in other words, the space available in which to write a message.

4. **Make several practice copies of the space.** Just put a piece of paper over the label and draw a quick (it can be messy) outline of the space.

5. **Practice writing the information within the space available and trying for balance.** At this point, don't worry about beautiful lettering; just think about size and spacing. Do several copies until you have a satisfactory arrangement.

6. **Refine the writing.** Once you get the approximate spacing, make a lined marking guide, following the directions in Chapter 5. I frequently use the generic marking guide provided on page 19, which gives $^{1}/_{2}$" and $^{1}/_{4}$" lines and centering lines. Place the practice paper label over the marking guide, and write the documentation information, centering and sizing to fit all letters in. Do this several times, if necessary.

7. **Practice on fabric.** This time, add whatever squiggles and flourishes on the letters you will want on the final label. Then, use the best copy as a marking guide.

8. **Write on the label.** Here are two options: Either you feel confident enough by now to write freehand but still use the marking guide for lines and spacing or you want to trace. Either way, anchor everything—the marking guide and the label—so nothing slips.

   Write freehand. Place the best practice label next to you as a guide for layout and size. Use the marking guide under the label for straight lines.
   Or trace. Go over key letters on the copy you are going to trace with a heavy marker so they show through the label. It is difficult to trace every letter, but key letters (usually uppercase ones) help you keep the sizing and spacing. Place the label over the guide label and trace the words.

9. **Write lightly the first time.** Then add contrast by going over the letters again.

   Note: To see the finished label, Leslie's Graduation, turn to page 33.

Chapter 5
The Marking Guide

Although some people can write directly on a label, most of us need some guidance in visualizing and planning the spacing of what we want to write. I was dissatisfied with pencil lines on my final fabric so I developed a tracing method. It is just like doing rough drafts for papers—you practice until you get it right; then you make the final copy. I have devised several ways for making this process easy, the most important of which is the marking guide.

The marking guide is a useful and easy-to-make piece of equipment for anyone who is going to write on fabric. You can make different ones for different projects, but I have provided a generic one for you on the facing page. The basic premise of the marking guide is that you can trace accurately if you have lines you can see when you lay the label over the guide.

HOW TO MAKE A FABRIC MARKING GUIDE

1. Cut a piece of muslin the same size or larger than your label.
2. Using a thick-pointed pen, draw lines on the muslin $1/2$" or $1/4$" apart. The width you choose might be determined by the particular label you are designing, or you can make a general set of lines as on page 19.
3. Anchor the guide to any smooth surface wih tape. Lay your label over the guide and tape. The lines will show through and the fabrics will stick together.

HOW TO USE THE FABRIC MARKING GUIDE

A fabric marking guide does several things: it provides a flat surface on which to write; it anchors your fabric because the muslin sticks to the label fabric; and, of course, it gives you guidelines so your writing can be straight and centered.

When you lay fabric over the marking guide, you can see the lines because you drew them in heavy pen, and, thus, you can use them to guide your writing. First, write on paper, then on practice fabric, and only when you are ready, on the final label.

WHEN A PAPER MARKING GUIDE IS USEFUL

I like the fabric marking guide because it anchors the fabric as it provides the lines for writing. The fabric on which I am writing clings to the guide underneath, which makes writing easy. Also, I use one general guide for many writing projects, so I like to have a generic one made up. You may find, however, for a one-time project, that you don't want such an elaborate guide. In that case, a paper marking guide will work well. It doesn't provide an anchor for the fabric, however, so you have to tape the layers down to avoid fabric slippage.

TRY A LIGHT BOX

The reason I developed the fabric marking guide is to avoid marking guidelines on my quilt label. The purpose of the thick lines is to eliminate the need for a light box or table. However, you may find a light box useful, if you have one. Lay a paper or fabric marking guide over the light box. Always anchor it well.

AN ADDED STEP

You may find that adding a step in the marking guide process helps you achieve perfect writing on the label:

1. Lay paper over the marking guide and practice centering and spacing the lettering until it looks the way you want it to look.

2. Once you have the layout of the lettering planned, make this copy into a traceable marking guide by going over the major elements with a heavy marker. If the lettering is tiny, you can't go over every letter, but it doesn't matter as long as you can see uppercase letters.

3. Use the second marking guide (the one with the lettering included) when you write on the practice fabric and on the real label.

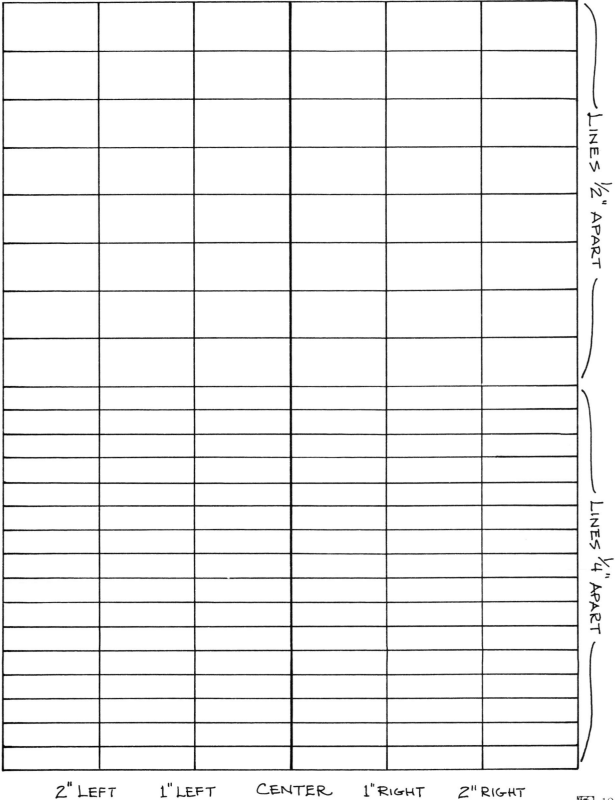

LINES ½" APART

LINES ¼" APART

2" LEFT   1" LEFT   CENTER   1" RIGHT   2" RIGHT

Chapter 6
Making Labels
Using Traceable Designs

A wonderful way to make a label is to draw designs or pictures with a permanent pen. You will already be writing the documentation information with the pen; a little practice will enable you to embellish the label with inkings. For those of us who are not artists (and I include myself in this category, which is why I developed the tracing methods described here), tracing provides an easy way to include beautiful designs on our labels.

Once you begin to look in magazines and books, you will see many lovely designs which are suitable for tracing. The secret, at least at first, is to keep it simple. Look for simple designs to trace. Many ads now have banners and pretty scrolls that can be traced. Articles sometimes have headings displayed in banners. Look, and you will see.

The pages of this book are also filled with line drawings, all of which are designed for you to trace. Take a moment to glance through the book. The ribbons and bows, flowers and bouquets, all can be incorporated into a label. As my gift to you, I have scattered traceable designs throughout the book. Try them.

HOW TO TRACE

Once you find a design you would like on your label, you are ready to trace. You can trace directly by placing the fabric over the design, or you may find a light box makes it easier.

Try tracing directly first. Place the fabric over the design. Can you see through the fabric well enough to see the outline of the design? The outline is all you actually need to trace. The rest you will fill in freehand. If you can't see the design through the fabric, place the open page and the fabric over a light box and trace.

INKING AND TRACING TECHNIQUES

Practice Makes Perfect! Have you heard this before? It applies to writing on fabric just as it does to everything else. You need to get the feel of the pen you are using on the particular fabric. Each pen writes differently on fabric than on paper and differently on different fabrics. Practice tracing techniques with scrap pieces of your actual label fabric. Actually, tracing on fabric is easier than on paper—the fabric is forgiving of mistakes, and glitches can usually be repaired.

1. **Trace or write lightly.** Whether you are drawing or writing, using a pattern or not, the first drawing should be very light. Use your finest-pointed pen. You can always go over a line again.

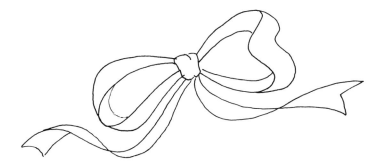

2. **To achieve a single pen stroke, you also need to practice drawing a long, unbroken line.** Any long line should look as if it were done in one pen stroke. I recommend starting to practice these strokes on paper, then going on to scrap fabric. In order to trace a long line without lifting the pen, study the line you will be tracing before you put pen to paper. I actually practice by moving my hand in the air, imitating the flow of the line before I begin. Place your hand in a position so that you can see the line ahead of you and can move the hand freely in a sweeping motion. For each of you, this position will be slightly different. Practice until you get the feel of a long, continuous pen line.

No   Yes

3. **Create contrast.** Since you are working in only one color, the contrast must be achieved in two ways: thick and thin lines as well as dark and light areas. Darken by going over lines a second time. The trick is to go over only some of the lines, so some lines remain delicate. As you do this, you will begin to achieve light and dark contrast. It doesn't matter which parts of the drawing you go over. I frequently choose curves or important

4. **Shade by using your pen on its side and very lightly to create sketchy lines.** When adding lines to pictures, work outward from the already-drawn lines. This way your heavier lines will be in the corners. Shade folds, curves, and corners.

5. **Stippling is done by holding the pen straight up and tapping the fabric ever so lightly.** It can be used for shading or as a final decoration outside the design. Used outside, it acts as a finishing touch, like a hint of baby's breath in a floral bouquet.

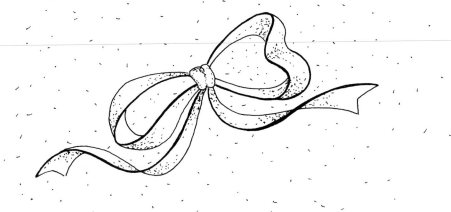

TRACING PROCEDURE

1. Trace lightly.
2. Trace only the outline. Don't try to get the thick-thin lines on the first drawing.
3. Remove the fabric and add the shading freehand, using the techniques just discussed.
4. Add your words where you want them. See Chapters 2, 3, and 4 for instructions on writing on fabric.

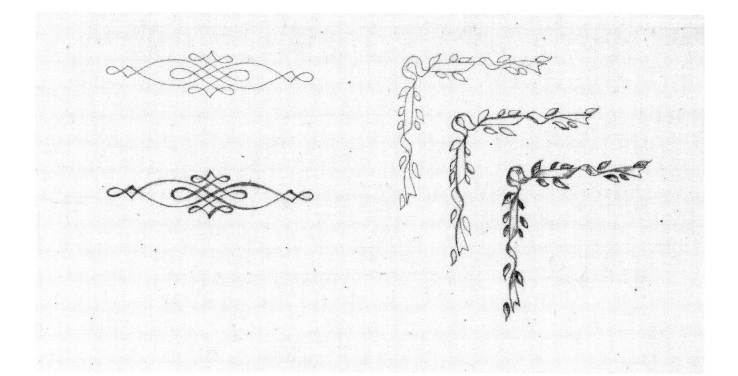

Chapter 7
Designs to Trace

On these pages are many traceable designs for you. There are several kinds: corner designs, top-bottom designs, and dingbats to go below, in between or beside words. Let's look at how these work.

CORNER DESIGNS

The corner designs are usable in the corners of any-sized labels. They are easily traceable—just trace one corner, then move and turn the label to trace the other corners.

For correct placement, mark the corners of your label. Make a paper version of your label and heavily mark the corner placement. Using a light box, lay the marked paper guide on the table first, then the traceable corner design, then the fabric label. Trace. Or mark the label corners with very light pencil lines or any disappearing marking pencil. This will eliminate one layer in the tracing, allowing you to work without a light box.

TOP AND BOTTOM CENTER DESIGNS

For a simple label, trace only a top or bottom design. Some lovely ones have been provided. A quick-and-easy way to mark the center of the label is to fold and press it. This gives you a center line. Or mark it with an erasable marker or make a marking guide as directed for the corner designs.

DINGBATS

Dingbats are lovely decorative swirls and squiggles to use as dividers between words or around words on your label. We frequently see such swirls on signed antique quilts, and they make wonderful finishing details. When you plan your label, plan space for a dingbat. Look at the labels shown in this book, and you will see how dingbats are used.

Made by
Ellen Hayes

August, 1993

Traceables

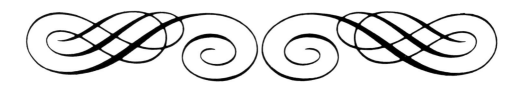

Chapter 8
Organizing Group Signings

Labeling a raffle, gift, or group quilt of any kind enhances its value, to say nothing of giving fame and glory to the makers! It is worth doing for every reason. Here are some suggestions to make sure that the skilled needlewomen involved in making your group quilt will sign it as beautifully as they quilted it.

When you want to have everyone in your group sign the label, you are confronted with special problems. Since everyone's signature is different in size and style, it is difficult to control how the label will look. Some careful planning will help.

STEPS TO FOLLOW

1. **Plan the size of your label.** A label may be of any size; it will not hurt the quilt to have a large label on the back. If you need to include 50 signatures plus documentation information, be generous in label size. I would say 8 ½" x 11" (standard typing paper size) should be adequate for most group quilt labels. Plan to use approximately one third of the label for the documentation information, leaving two thirds for signing. At right is a sample marking guide.

2. **Decide on the fabric.** Whenever possible, use a fabric that was also used on the quilt front, one that will look nice against the backing you have chosen, and that is light enough in color to show the writing well. Since you will be providing the pen and supervising the signing, pretest the fabric with the pen you plan to use for the signing. Test with prewashed fabric for bleeding and washability. It is crucial to know how much the pen bleeds because different hands have different writing techniques— slow, quick, dragging, hurried—and you **can't** control this during the signing. Choose a pen and point size that work best on your fabric.

   Cut lots of extra pieces of the chosen fabric so each signer can practice before signing the actual label. Ask your best writer to experiment writing the documentation information on paper, using the directions for centering and lettering given in Chapters 3 and 4.

3. **Design the label,** using the suggestions in Chapter 1.

4. **Design a marking guide customized for your signers.** See pages 18 and 19 for

Rose of Sharon made by the members of The Annapolis Quilt Guild for raffle at the 1992 Quilt Show June 13, 1993

⅓

⅔

directions on making a marking guide, but customize it in this way: On paper, make a line-only marking guide. For 50 signatures, on two thirds of an 8 ½" x 11" sheet, plan 25 lines with two signatures per line. (For 60, plan 30 lines, etc.) Look at the sample marking guide below. Include a vertical line down the middle so signers know how much space they actually have.

5. **Transfer the marking guide onto muslin and onto foam core.** When working with many writers, the fabric marking guide instead of paper is worth the effort—it helps anchor the label. Attach the muslin marking guide onto a foam core board that is covered with a layer of flannel.

6. **Make the label.**

7. **Decorate the label.**

8. **Have the master writer write the documentation information.**

9. **Plan your signing party.**

THE GROUP SIGNING PARTY

Get your group together for the signing if at all possible. Passing the label around from house to house is too dangerous; anything can happen from tea stains to ballpoint pen marks to a lost label! Try feeding your signers after the signing as an incentive to get them to come. Having all sign at the same time will save you hours of hassle. At the signing party, do this:

1. **Explain to the signers how the label is set up and how you want them to sign.** Explain how and where on the label to sign and the idiosyncrasies of the pen they will use.

2. **Show them the marking guide on its foam core back, how you will put the label over it, and that you can see through it.**

3. **Pass around the pen and a sample piece of the actual fabric pinned over the marking guide.** Let each person practice writing on this sample.

4. **Pin the actual label over the marking guide carefully.**

5. **Invite the signers to come up to a front table to sign.** Have a "supervisor" there to show them the right places to sign. I suggest filling a line across before moving down rather than filling the left column and then moving to the right. This way, if there are fewer signers than planned, the extra space is left evenly at the bottom and can be filled with a lovely inked dingbat or scroll.

Yes		No	
1	2	1	11
3	4	2	12
5	6	3	
7	8	4	
9	10	5	
11	12	6	
		7	
		8	
		9	
		10	

6. **Add the names of those who are absent after all those present have signed.**

7. **Appliqué the label to the quilt backing.** Trim away the backing behind the label.

8. **Baste, quilt, and bind the quilt as usual.**

   Note: You can present a half-hour lesson on embellishing handwriting if your group wants it. See Chapter 3 for tips on fancy handwriting or refer to *Friendship's Offering* by the author for more information.

Part Three

The Labels

Chapter 9
Quick but Effective Labels
designed by Susan McKelvey

The label you make need not be elaborate to be showy. There are many quick ways to decorate a label. Consider some of the methods described here.

STRIPES

Frame the label with a stripe. Any width of stripe—but probably narrow—may be cut from any striped fabric. If you have used a stripe somewhere on your quilt top, try it as your label frame. Decide on the size of your label. Measure its perimeter. Sew the border on with the sewing machine.

PRETEND PIECED BORDERS (Color photograph on page 34)

Look at fabric with an eye for a design adaptable for borders. When cut out and sewn onto a label, many prints will look pieced. With a checked print, you won't even need to miter.

PREPRINTED MEDALLIONS (*Christmas Fawn* on page 34 and *Heart Medallion* on page 35)

Look at preprinted fabrics as labels. Many are now being printed to look like blocks. All are adaptable to your purposes as quick but showy labels.

QUICK BRODERIE PERSE (*Leslie's Graduation* on page 33 and *Quick Strawberries* on page 34)

Choose any pictorial elements from a fabric, preferably one used on the quilt front, and appliqué just a few onto the label. Upper left and lower right corners are good places. This echoes the front and is very quick. The fish on Leslie's Graduation label were cut out and appliquéd onto the label.

RIBBON

Use any elegant ribbon as a border. This has the added advantage of avoiding frayed edges and creating easy appliqué. The ribbon may be added easily with the sewing machine or by hand.

LACE

Use lace the same way that you would ribbon. Just attach it on the edges. You may want to embellish further, but for a quick label, just the lace makes a fragile yet finished border. Attach it so it folds out from the label and covers the backing or so it folds in over the label. Tacking the loose edge of the lace will protect it.

PREPRINTED LABELS (*Memories of Home* on page 35)

Use a preprinted label. Then all you need to do is write the documentation on it and appliqué it onto the quilt backing. The label shown is silkscreened. I designed it as an easy, attractive label for use on any quilt. See **Sources** for more information.

Chapter 10
Paper-Folded Borders for Labels
designed by Susan McKelvey

Paper-folded borders are easy to make and provide charming frames for labels. It is easier to appliqué the label to the quilt if you design the label with the outer edge straight and the fancy cutwork edge facing inward toward the label. Several label frames designed by using the paper-fold method are included, but you can easily design your own cutwork label, too.

DESIGN YOUR OWN PAPER-FOLDED BORDERS

1. Choose a size and shape for the label. Squares are easier to do because all sides are cut in exactly the same way. The rectangular shape is a bit more difficult because the bottom and top edges are different from the sides, and, therefore, they require a different design and refolding.

2. Cut several pieces of paper the size of the finished label.

3. Fold one sheet of paper in half and then in fourths:

4. Fold the corner at a 45° angle. Be sure to fold in from the outer corners (loose edges) rather than out from the center (folded edges). If the label is a square, simply fold on the diagonal. If the label is a rectangle, you will have a leftover section after you have folded the 45° angle.

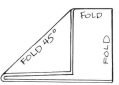

5. Mark the outer points (loose corners) with a star or other symbol to avoid confusion later when unfolding and refolding.

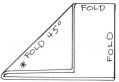

6. To draw designs, work on only one half or one quarter of the label, but to avoid confusion, unfold the paper so you can visualize the entire label. Mark the folded diagonal lines with pencil if you need to see them. Consider the outer ¹/₂" as the border—you know that you want border fabric there. Mark it off.

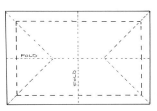

7. Begin by designing only one corner with a shape pointing inward toward the center. Don't worry if it goes over the marked border line. This can be changed. To maximize design space, try a different design in each corner (even though eventually you'll choose only one design).

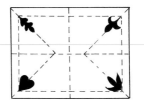

8. When you have a corner design you think you might like, go on to the next step—altering the border shape so it isn't just straight lines and so it doesn't interfere with the corner design. An S curve is always attractive (see page 13).

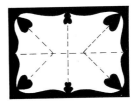

9. With a rectangular shape, you may want a center design on the longer sides as well as at the corners. Try drawing one.

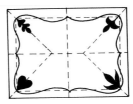

10. When you have a likely design, refold the paper and cut all four sections at the same time. Open and evaluate critically for several things:
    ♦ Is it too difficult to appliqué? If so, simplify it.
    ♦ Can you get into and turn under every area? If not, redesign.
    ♦ Is it attractive?
11. Paper is cheap, and cutting is easy, so cut several variations of a design until you come up with a satisfactory one.

⬛⬛⬛ Cutting Supplies ⬛⬛⬛

Paper: For designing, folding, and cutting, any inexpensive typing paper is fine. For accuracy on the final cut, tracing paper is best.

Scissors: Use a pair of scissors reserved for paper cutting. They must be sharp and have two pointed tips. I use good-quality embroidery scissors, but cutting paper ruins them for cutting thread, so label them for paper cutting only.

USING THE PAPER-FOLDED BORDERS PROVIDED

General Considerations

1. The borders in this book are 5" x 7" rectangles, but each is easily adaptable to any size.
2. Squares are easier to make because when you design a corner, it is exactly one fourth of the design. The rectangular shape is a little more difficult because the bottom edge is a different length from the side and, therefore, requires a different design.
3. The designs for the borders are given in full size. The section you need to copy before folding is marked off with dotted lines.
4. To adapt to a square label, trace only the corner and one side of the design. The short side will make a 5" square label, and the long side will make a 7" square label.

Transferring the Border Design From the Book to the Paper

Measure and cut a piece of paper (tracing paper makes it more accurate) the size of your label. Fold as in Steps 3 and 4 on page 29. Unfold the paper. Lay it over the line drawing and trace only one section. Refold. Cut all four layers at the same time. *Note:* You need to refold twice: First, refold all the way and cut the corner section. Then unfold to half and cut the sides and bottom. Because they are different, you must be careful here.

Transferring the Border Design From the Paper to the Fabric

There are several ways to transfer the designs from paper to fabric; which one you choose depends on the way you will appliqué. Turn now to page 51 to help you decide how you will appliqué and for directions on how to transfer the border designs to fabric. When you are ready to transfer the border designs, there are some things to keep in mind:

1. In all appliqué methods, leave the outer edge of the border unmarked and cut the fabric an extra 1" to 2" larger than the outer edge of the paper pattern. In this way you include the seam allowance for sewing the label onto the quilt and a generous allowance for adjustment and straightening after sewing the label together.
2. If you are doing needle-turned appliqué, cut only 2" ahead of your sewing. In order to center the border on the background fabric, you must cut out some fabric in the center, but cut out just enough to center; don't trim to the ¼" seam allowance until you are within inches of sewing that area. This prevents the fraying of delicate edges.

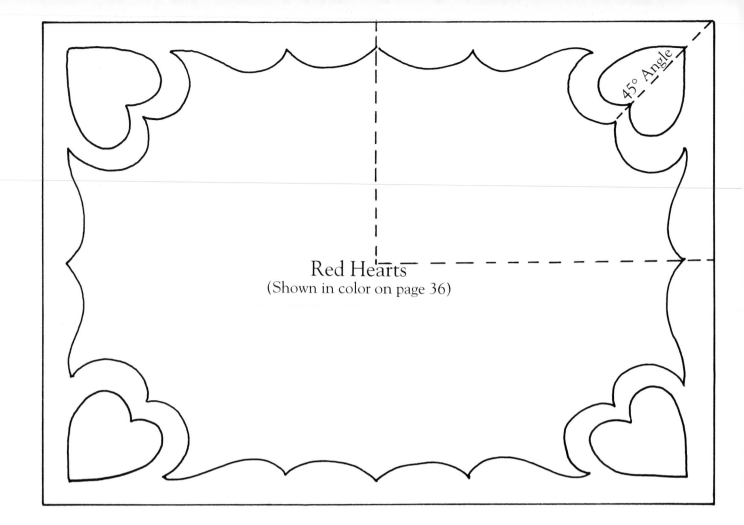

Red Hearts
(Shown in color on page 36)

45° Angle

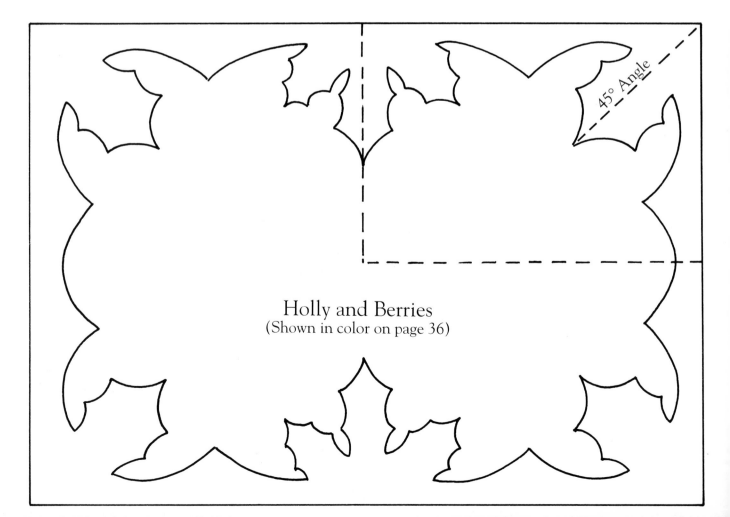

Holly and Berries
(Shown in color on page 36)

45° Angle

To
Leslie M. McKelvey

Upon her Graduation
from the University of Michigan

May 1992

Signed by her Sisters of A Δ π

With Love
from
Mom

Millersville, Md.
1991 – 1992

Leslie's Graduation by Susan McKelvey. In this example of quick *broderie perse*, the fish were cut from printed fabric and appliquéd onto the blue background.
Note: The documentation on all labels is inked with the Pigma .01 pen unless otherwise noted.

Pretend Pieced Border by Susan McKelvey uses an allover checked fabric cut into strips to make an easy label border.

Merry Christmas
Andrea
From
Mom & Dad
December 25, 1992
Troy, Michigan

Christmas Fawn by Susan McKelvey. The fawn was cut from the center of the preprinted medallion, appliquéd into the corner, and replaced with plain fabric on which to write.

Quick *Broderie Perse* Strawberries by Susan McKelvey. A quick label made from printed motifs appliquéd onto a background. Documentation inked with the Callipen.

"Memories of Childhood"
Made in 1992
By Ellen Hadlin
For my daughter, Joan Hadlin
Upon her graduation from
Old Mill High School

This Album Quilt was
made by the members
of the
Appleton Quilt Guild
Appleton, Wisc...
April 199...

Traced Corners by Susan McKelvey is traced from a design on page 24. The delicate pale gold fabric adds refinement to the simple label.

Age enricheth true love,
Like noble wine.
Gerald Massey

Happy 50th Anniversary
Henry & Henrietta Dobson
April 6, 1993

from all of your children and grandchildren

Heart Medallion by Susan McKelvey is a preprinted medallion in which the flowers were cut from the center and scattered along the heart's edge while plain fabric was appliquéd into the center.

To
Sarah & Adam Pike
Best Wishes in your
New Home.

"Home is where the heart is."
Pliny the Elder

From Louise & Ben
Lindenmyer

May 11, 1993
Homewood, Ill.

Memories of Home is a silkscreened label designed by Susan McKelvey and available from her company, Wallflower Designs.

"Spinning Vision"
A variation on a traditional
Kaleidoscope block made by
Emory Jedlicka of Beaufort, N.C.
Begun in March, 1991 and
finished in May 1992.

Red Hearts by Susan McKelvey is a paper-folded border design, which provides lots of space for label information.

"Childhood Memories"
Made for Helen Meyers Payne
by her mother,
Evelyn Wilson Meyers

December 25, 1993   Omaha, Nebraska

Holly and Berries by Susan McKelvey is a paper-folded border design, which provides lots of space for label information.

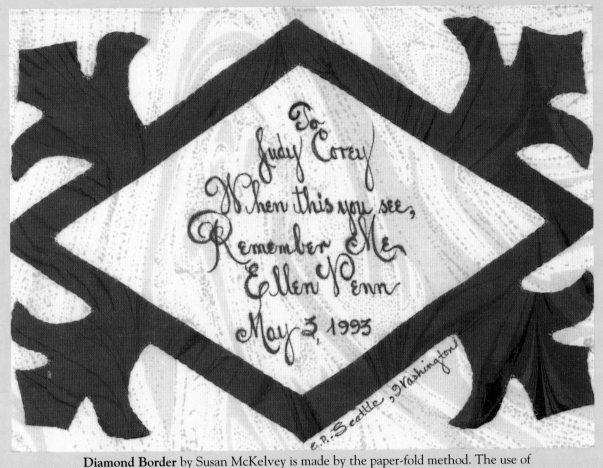

Diamond Border by Susan McKelvey is made by the paper-fold method. The use of marbled background fabic adds interest.

To
Judy Corey
When this you see,
Remember Me
Ellen Penn
May 3, 1993

E.P. Seattle, Washington

To Daniel England

From India Jacobsen

"I will wear my heart upon my sleeve."
Shakespeare
February, 1993

Blue Border by Susan McKelvey uses paper-fold methods to make an elaborate label. Using striped fabric for the background insures straight writing.

Rose Oval by Dawnell Reeves makes an exquisite label and is the inspiration for the book cover. Notice the hand-dyed fabrics used for the flowers and ribbon.

Basket of Flowers by Dawnell Reeves inspires us to think of alternatives to outside borders.

Baby Bears by Rhoda Miller. Rhoda appliquéd two facing bears on either side of the label. This is a good layout and may be used with any technique from appliqué to stamping.

Heart and Pansies by Dawnell Reeves combines hand-dyed fabrics and lace in an elegant label. The printed fabric makes an interesting background.

Filigree Border by Dawnell Reeves provides an area in which to write and a border to which any flowers or bows may be added.

Happy Birthday, Margaret
May flowers of love
Around thee be twined,
And the sunshine of peace
Shed its joy o're thy mind.

Your Friend,
Lynn
September 9, 1992

Trailing Roses by Pele Fleming. Pele first stamped the roses with black ink and then colored them with fabric dye pens, making a colorful and quick label.

This quilt was made for
Thomas England Bolton
upon his birth, July 16, 1993
to Scott and Karen Bolton
of Iowa City, Iowa

Love from Grandma Jo
Josephine McLaren
North Liberty, Iowa

Cat Watching by Pele Fleming. The cats and moons were stamped, then colored with fabric dye pens. The layout is particularly nice and adaptable to other motifs.

A friendship quilt for
Carla Conte

From the seven friends in
her evening bee.
                                June
                                1993

Baby Birds by Pele Fleming. Stamped in two corners and then colored, this cheerful label is easy to create and fun to use.

To
Heinz and Ingrid
From

Susan and Doug

Remember Us from Afar
Millersville, Maryland
1993

Strawberries by Anna Macaluso is painted in acrylics and exemplifies how effective using two corners can be.

Handmade by Anna Macaluso
Totowa N. J.

Pansies with Ribbon by Anna Macaluso was painted in acrylics on muslin. The layout of centering the strong upper design and repeating it in a smaller version below the writing is easily adapted to any of the other techniques described in this book.

Grandmother's Flower Garden
Made by Emily Grange
In the year of 1993
Annapolis, Maryland

Field of Flowers by Anna Macaluso was painted in acrylics and is a pretty layout, placing the design at the bottom trailing upward around the writing.

Grandmother's Flower Garden

Made from antique scraps found in my Grandmother's attic.

Meg Mulroy ♥ Ludington, Michigan ♥ 1993

Geraniums by Pauline Trout. A single flower in the upper left corner leaves lots of space for writing.

Ariels' Stars

This quilt is an original design by Ariel Payne.

Finished in July of 1992.

Asheville, North Carolina.

Purple Mums by Pauline Trout. The same left placement of the drawn flowers is effective.
For inking technique, notice the irregular squiggles for leaves and petals.

Floral Bouquet by Jackie Janovsky. Ribbon, beads, and embroidery floss are combined in this label, which is detailed but still leaves room for writing. The design is adaptable to inking, and the ribbon strips could be incorporated into any label.

Maria's Roses by Sandy Flores. Sandy used the two-corner layout for her Brazilian embroidered label. This design is adaptable to inking, painting, or silk ribbon embroidery.

Love Bird Wreath by Susan McKelvey combines stenciling with fine detailing in acrylic paint and Pigma pen to make a quick but beautiful label.

Stenciled Boughs by Nancy Tribolet. The delicate border, stenciled in green and rust, surrounds the writing and is outlined with the brown Pigma pen, which adds depth and detail.

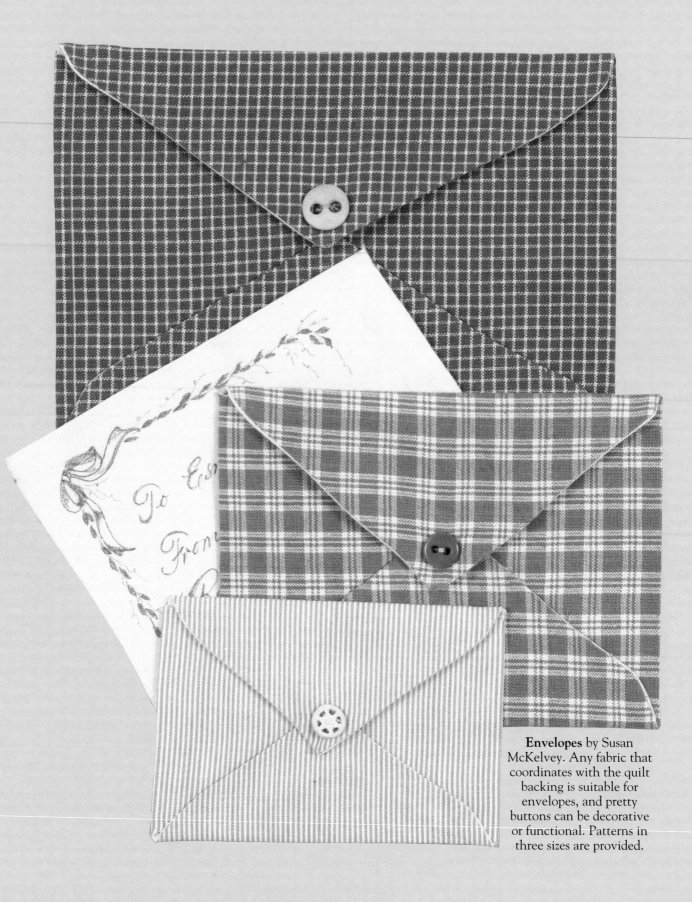

Envelopes by Susan McKelvey. Any fabric that coordinates with the quilt backing is suitable for envelopes, and pretty buttons can be decorative or functional. Patterns in three sizes are provided.

Dear Aunt Emmy,

I made this

scra... you

Bec...

19

19

**Envelopes
and Label**
by Susan McKelvey.
Ribbon and
porcelain buttons
decorate these
envelopes. The
inner linings and
label border are
inked with traceable
designs available in
this book.

Wedding Label designed by Susan McKelvey and printed by Fabric Fotos. This stunning label for a special occasion was made using two transfer techniques: a copy machine and heat transfer.

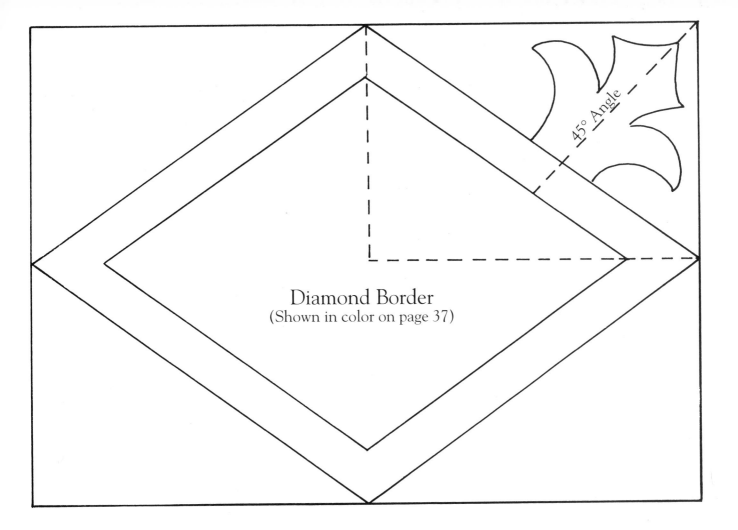

Diamond Border
(Shown in color on page 37)

45° Angle

Blue Border
(Shown in color on page 37)

Chapter 11
Hand-Appliquéd Labels and Techniques

designed by Dawnell Reeves and Rhoda Miller

As we have discussed in other chapters, appliqué is an easy way to apply a decorative element to a label. You may appliqué a border (as in Chapter 10) or a single element (as in Chapter 9). You may also create an appliqué design just for the label.

The exquisite floral labels in this chapter have been custom-designed for us by Dawnell Reeves, a talented artist who, with her partner Carol Shoaf, has turned her interest in appliqué into a pattern business called Legacy in Stitches. After seeing their appliqué designs, I asked them to design some labels for this book. The five charming labels on the following pages are the result.

Notice as you examine these labels that the elements are easily adaptable to any size or shape label. Ribbons, bows, and flowers—all are movable and interchangeable. The ribbons and flowers could go at the top or bottom, on the left or right of a label. By providing you with several types of flowers, Dawnell has created endless possibilities for varying any label by making larger bouquets or combining and mixing flowers.

What makes these labels look so fragile, delicate, and realistic is the use of hand-dyed and hand-marbled fabrics. These fabrics give the shaded modulation of folded ribbon and real flowers. You can learn a great deal about how to color your own appliqué work by examining the photographs of the labels on pages 38 and 39. Suppliers for such exquisite fabrics are listed under **Sources.**

The cover designs, also designed by Dawnell, are given here in a 5" x 7" format.

The Baby Bear label was designed by Rhoda Miller, a quilter and bear designer from Annapolis, Maryland. The bears, which are placed at the right and left sides of Rhoda's label, could be moved easily. In any position, they would make a charming label for a child's quilt.

There are many appliqué methods. Read on for a discussion of hand-appliqué techniques.

Appliqué Supplies

freezer paper

scissors: paper and fabric

appliqué needles (any long, slender needle; milliner's, sharps in 10-12; Dawnell prefers betweens. Personal preference rules here.)

background fabric

fabric for appliqué elements

thread that matches appliqué fabrics: If you can't match exactly, choose a darker thread.

fabric marker for marking turn lines: Many markers are on the market designed especially for marking fabric, but the Pigma pen is wonderful for marking turn and placement lines. I use the .01 (very fine) to draw fold lines for hand appliqué. It makes a very narrow line, which is easily hidden when turned under. It shows up on medium-dark fabrics such as turkey red and dark green; it doesn't disappear if you are appliquéing over a long period of time; and it doesn't bleed when the quilt is washed later. It's great!

Transferring the Design From the Paper to the Fabric for Hand Appliqué

There are several ways to transfer the designs from paper to fabric. Which one you choose depends on the way you will appliqué. Here are three transfer methods. Choose the one that best suits you.

Method 1: Turn Lines Drawn on Top of the Appliqué Fabric

Make a pattern for each appliqué piece. Lay the pattern over the fabric and pin well. Mark the turn line, leaving room to add $^3/_{16}$" seam allowances on all patches. Baste the seam allowance under or leave it free for needle-turning-as-you-go.

Method 2: Freezer Paper on Top of the Appliqué

1. Transfer the traced and cut paper pattern to freezer paper. Either lay the freezer paper over the pattern, dull side up (a light box helps here), or glue the pattern piece to the dull side of the freezer paper. Draw the turn lines on the freezer paper with a Pigma pen. Cut out the freezer paper pattern.

2. Iron the freezer paper pattern onto the top of the fabric, shiny side to the front of the fabric. There are two ways to hand appliqué with the freezer paper on top. In the first, leave the freezer paper ironed on the fabric and use its edges to show you the turn lines as you go. Many people use this method successfully. I must be very sloppy in handling the paper-fabric appliqué piece because I find that the freezer paper peels off and leaves me with no line to guide me. So I take one further step: Using the ironed-on freezer paper as a pattern, I mark the turn lines with a Pigma pen. I then remove the freezer paper and keep it nearby as an exact pattern, but I use the drawn turn line while appliquéing.

Method 3: Freezer Paper on the Back of the Appliqué

1. Mark or glue the paper pattern onto the dull side of the freezer paper as in Step 1 of Method 2, but remember that because you are applying the pattern to the back of the fabric, it must be reversed. Therefore, when tracing the pattern onto the freezer paper, turn either the pattern or the freezer paper over.

2. Iron the freezer paper onto the back of the fabric, shiny side of the paper to the **back** of the fabric.

3. Cut out the piece, leaving a $^3/_{16}$" to $^1/_4$" seam allowance.

4. Using tiny, pointed scissors and a glue stick, turn and glue the fabric seam allowance to the freezer paper. You will have to clip some, but *clip as little as possible.* This will give you a glue-basted edge for appliquéing.

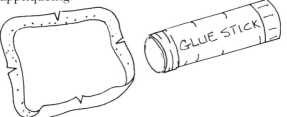

5. Lay the glue-basted piece onto the background fabric, pin, and appliqué.

6. After appliquéing, remove the freezer paper by clipping from the back, moistening the glue and paper with a damp cloth, and pulling it out.

General Instructions for Needle-turned Appliqué

With needle-turned appliqué, you don't fold the seam allowance under until you get to it as you sew. Use the side of the needle to guide the seam allowance under about 1" to 2" ahead of you. Anchor it with a pin at the farthest point turned. In between, either pin it, or needle-turn to the exact position as you go.

1. Position the element to be appliquéd and pin just enough to anchor. You don't need to thread baste.

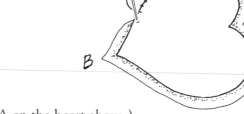

2. Use tiny tacking stitches and a slender needle.

3. Start at an easy curve (such as Point A on the heart above.).

4. There are two kinds of points: outside and inside (Point B on the heart is an outside point and Point C is an inside one).

5. On an outside point like B, do not clip. Needle-turn the fabric ahead of your sewing, and sew all the way to the point. Take an extra stitch at the point. Then turn the entire element, using the side of your needle to turn the fabric under and tuck it in, and continue stitching.

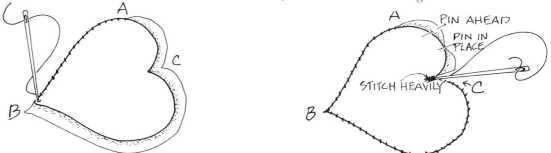

6. On an inside point like C, sew as close to the point as you can before the fabric interferes. Then clip into the point—one clip. Pin the far side down so it stays out of your way and doesn't get rubbed, and sew into the point. Turn the fabric and needle-turn the first inch of the second side under. Take many tiny stitches on both sides of the point to keep the fabric from fraying. Then continue up the other side with the regular stitch.

ON APPLIQUÉING PRE-BASTED OR GLUED PIECES

To smooth the edges: As you turned and glued or basted, some edges may not have been turned under perfectly smoothly. Use the needle as you appliqué to loosen and smooth out these imperfect curves.

APPLIQUÉING MULTI-LAYERED FLOWERS

The numbers on the patterns indicate the order in which to appliqué the pieces and help you locate and place the pieces quickly. Either freezer paper method makes numbering easy.

APPLIQUÉ STYLE

I find that appliquéing "over the bottom edge" of the appliqué element rather than over the top edge gives me better vision of the edge and, thus, better control as I turn it under. This method works especially well for complicated, multi-layered appliqué projects. Look at the diagrams below. Perhaps you might want to try "over the bottom edge" appliqué, too.

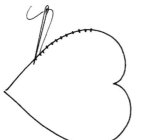

Over the Top
Hold heart like this. You look over upper edge. Turn line and seam allowance is rolled away from your vision.

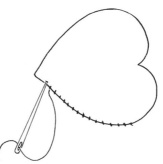

Over the Bottom
Hold heart like this. You look over bottom edge. You can see the turn line and seam allowance well.

Basket of Flowers
(Shown in color on page 38)

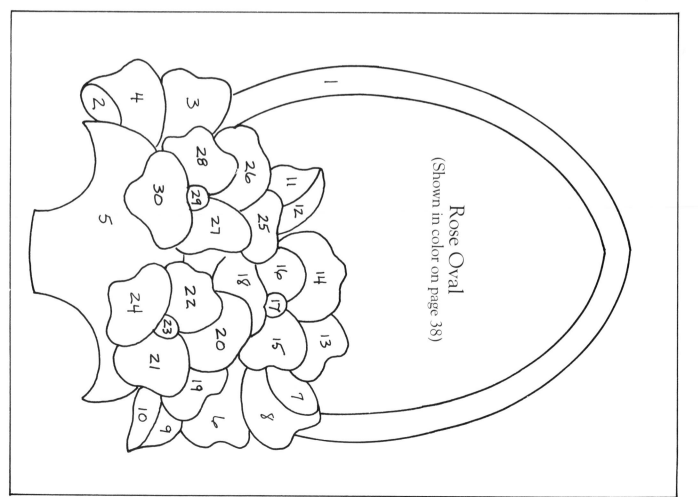

Rose Oval
(Shown in color on page 38)

Heart and Pansies
(Shown in color on page 39)

Filigree Border
(Shown in color on page 39)

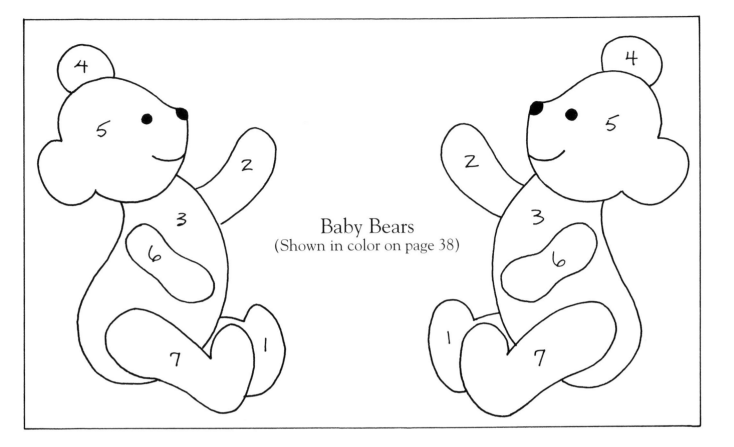

Baby Bears
(Shown in color on page 38)

Rose and Ribbon
(Shown in color on back cover)

Chapter 12
Stamped Labels
designed by Pele Fleming

Stamping is a versatile and easy way to create attractive labels. It provides a quick way to apply images to fabric. You can repeat one image, and you can change its placement. Use any of the design layouts discussed in Chapter 1. One stamp provides a multitude of design options. Stamping is fun and limited only by your creativity!

The most exciting stamps I have found for textile stamping are made by Pele Fleming, who offers stamping supplies through her company, Pelle's. Unlike most available rubber stamps, which are designed for paper stamping, Pelle's See-Thru™ stamps are designed as textile stamps. They are acrylic rather than rubber, have deep indentations that allow you to print fine lines, and are mounted on plastic rather than wood, which allows you to see through the stamp for perfect placement. Pele also has designed a special stamp pad, and she supplies a permanent ink, which comes in numerous colors and leaves the fabric soft and pliable.

All of the stamped labels shown were done by Pele Fleming, using her stamps, ink, and pad. From cats to roses, all of Pele's labels have a free and delightful quality, full of humor and panache.

A stamped label may be left plain, in which case it looks much like an inked label in one color. Or, after stamping, the label may be colored with fabric markers or pens. Also, you can combine stamping and freehand drawing.

Stamping Supplies

fabric
ink
stamp pad
small spatula or plastic knife
stamp

STAMPING DIRECTIONS

1. Prewash and iron the label fabric. Cut plenty of extra fabric pieces for practice.
2. Stamp on a hard, flat surface. Place a layer or two of fabric under the fabric to be stamped, but keep it flat and smooth.
3. Use Pelle's stamp pad—it is especially designed for good ink dispersement.
4. Ink the pad slowly, working the ink into the pad with the knife. If there are globs of ink on the pad, scrape them off. Re-ink when the pad gets too dry.
5. Ink the stamp by tapping it gently and repeatedly on the ink pad until you see that the entire image to be stamped shines with ink. This is easy to see because the stamp is clear and no matter what color the ink, it shows up on the surface. Don't press too hard on the pad because too much ink will cause a blur when stamping.
6. Stamp the fabric by pressing down firmly without moving the stamp. Press evenly. If part of the image doesn't stamp, try again, using more even pressure. The advantage of the See Thru™ stamps is that you can get direct pressure onto every part of the stamp.
7. Practice makes perfect. After a few tries, you will know the right amount of ink and pressure to apply to achieve a good image.

8. Touch up: I have found that the Pigma pen is wonderful for touching up an almost perfect line. On one label, I had four almost-perfect corners stamped; they were straight and clear. I didn't want to do them again, but several lines were slightly broken. I touched them up with the Pigma black pen, and they looked perfect.

9. Clean-up of the stamps: Wipe off with alcohol-free baby wipes or similar wipes. If the ink dries on the stamp, wash with warm water.

10. Care and cleaning of the stamp pad: After stamping, if you are going to be stamping again within a week and don't want to waste the ink already in the pad, simply put the pad in an air-tight plastic bag and store in the refrigerator. This will keep it moist until you are going to stamp again. When ready to re-use, just add more ink, if necessary. To clean the pad, rinse out with warm water and squeeze gently. Don't let ink dry on the pad because the pad will become hard, and it will no longer be usable.

Chapter 13
Embroidered Labels

designed by Jackie Janovsky and Sandy Flores

Embroidery is a time-honored decorative technique for many small projects. Why not consider it for a quilt label? Whether you use traditional embroidery floss, silk ribbon, or rayon thread, add beads or buttons, the many border and vine designs available for embroidery can be adapted easily to quilt labels. The labels included here were designed by Jackie Janovsky of Annapolis, Maryland, who specializes in making and teaching embroidery and other needlework, and by Sandy Flores of Sebastopol, California, a teacher and designer of Brazilian embroidery.

In Floral Bouquet, Jackie has used a variety of techniques including laid-on ribbon, embroidery with floss and silk ribbon, and beading. Sandy has used several basic stitches in her delicate Brazilian embroidered label called Maria's Roses. What makes Brazilian embroidery unique is the use of shiny rayon thread and wrapping stitches to build up a three-dimensional look. Although these labels show only a sampling of the many embroidery stitches available, we hope they will inspire you to try others on your quilt labels.

DIRECTIONS FOR MAKING JACKIE'S FLORAL BOUQUET LABEL

> **Embroidery Supplies for Jackie's Floral Bouquet Label**
>
> $1/4$"-wide ribbon (silk, satin or rayon): baby blue
> $1/16$"-wide rayon ribbon: in a matching color
> $1/4$"-wide ribbon: green for leaves
> six purchased ribbon rosettes: two deep rose and four pale pink
> $1/8$"-wide silk ribbon: medium rose
> pearl beads
> embroidery floss: green
> embroidery needle

1. Using the label drawing provided, sew the $1/4$" baby blue ribbon onto the label by machine or hand about 1" inside the outer edges.
2. In pencil, lightly trace the embroidery lines for the trailing vine, embroidered leaves, and rosette placement.
3. With two strands of green floss, embroider the vines and leaves.
   a. Vines: Use a stem stitch and work from the left to the right, keeping the needle to the left of the thread.

b. Small leaves: Use a satin stitch and work straight stitches along the shape as shown, entering at the same two points (A and B).

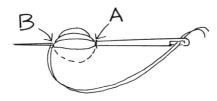

c. Large Leaves: Using two strands of floss, work the leaves in a herringbone stitch. Bring the needle up at A and down at B to the right of the center line and up again at C to the left of the center line. Then take the needle down at D and up at E. Repeat these steps until the leaf is filled in.

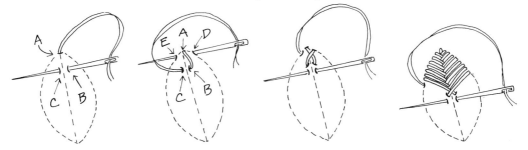

4. Roses. Use purchased silk rosettes. Sew them in place.
5. Buds: Use the pink silk ribbon and the colonial knot stitch.
   a. Grasp the ribbon 3" from the exit hole and pull toward your body.
   b. Lay the needle on top of the 3" of ribbon, slip the point of the needle under the ribbon, and pull to the left.
   c. Loop the ribbon over and under the needle to form a figure 8.
   d. Thread the ribbon back into the fabric near its exit point. Pull the knot snugly against the needle and fabric as you pull it through the fabric.

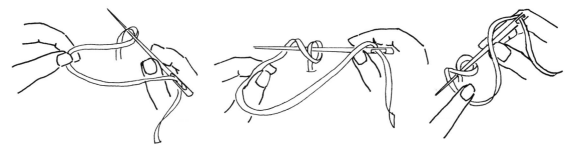

6. Rose Buds: Use the pink silk ribbon and the lazy daisy stitch.

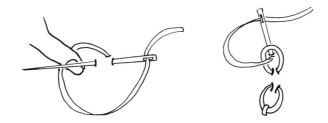

7. Green Ribbon Leaves: Using the green ribbon, make four ¹/₂" loops. Tuck them in behind the rosettes, and tack them in place.

8. Ribbon Loops: Using the ¹/₁₆" blue ribbon, make several loops each about ¹/₂" long and secure them at their base with a few stitches. Tack them just above the bouquet.

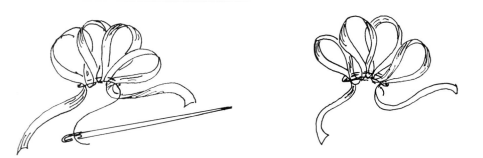

9. Using white sewing thread, add the seed pearls.

DIRECTIONS FOR MAKING SANDY'S LABEL, MARIA'S ROSES

1. Trace the design onto the label fabric with light pencil lines or a disappearing marker.
2. The Rose:
   a. Divide the circle of the rose into four equal parts.

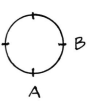

   b. Bring the needle up at point A, down at B, and back up at A, pushing the needle through almost to the eye of the needle.

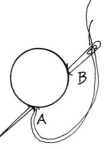

c. Using a cast-on stitch, cast on eight stitches.

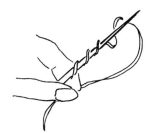

d. Pull the needle through at B and come up at C. This completes the first petal.

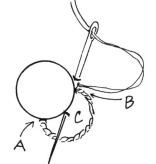

e. Continue making petals clockwise around the circle, always starting the next petal in the center of the last petal, going down at the next dot, and back up at A. For each petal, cast on two more loops (8-10-12-14-16-18-20-22-24) until you reach 24. Continue with 24 cast-on stitches until the rose looks full.

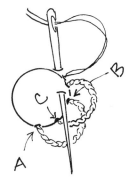

3. Rose Buds: These are eight-wrap bullion stitches with a 10- or 12-wrap cast-on stitch around it. Underneath, it is a 12-wrap bullion stitch in green for the calyx and a stem stitch.

4. Vines: Use the stem stitch given in step 3 for the Floral Bouquet Label directions.

5. Leaves:

   a. The small leaves are one straight stitch with four alternating stitches around it. With the tip of the leaf (A) pointing away from you, come up at the tip and go down at the base (B) of the leaf.

   b. For the larger leaves, follow the instructions for the small leaf but make the first stitch a little shorter than the length of the leaf. On alternating sides, fill in with a satin stitch, always going down at the base of the leaf.

Floral Bouquet
(Shown in color on page 44)

KEY:

ⓖ	Purchased Rosettes
ⓨ	Silk Ribbon Rosebuds Colonial Knots
∴	Pearl Beads
🍃	Large Leaves
🍃	Small Leaves
🍃	Silk Ribbon in Lazy Daisy

KEY:

🌹	Bullion Rose
🍃	Rosebuds
⌖	Vines
🍃	Small Leaves
🍃	Large Leaves

Maria's Roses
(Shown in color on page 44)

Chapter 14
Labels Painted With Acrylics
designed by Anna Macaluso

For those of you who want to paint your labels, Anna Macaluso, a quilt artist from New Jersey, has designed some lovely borders for you to try. These labels are painted in acrylic paint, which is totally washable and makes a bright, colorful label. The designs are also perfectly adaptable to tracing or coloring with permanent pens or fabric markers.

Supplies Needed

pencil: for tracing
label abric: prewashed and ironed
small brush: Anna recommends the Grumbacher 626-B
acrylic paint: dark green, bright green; black, white; purple, red, blue, yellow
optional: light box

GENERAL PAINTING DIRECTIONS:

1. Trace the design onto the label fabric, using a #2 pencil and light box if necessary.
2. When painting, do not overly blend colors. Color mixing may be done directly on fabric.
3. Paint the vines and leaves first, using bright green.
4. Shade using a dark green or black.
5. Highlight with white (see the ribbon folds in color in *Pansies with Ribbon*, page 42). This gives a three-dimensional effect.
6. Use the point of the brush to paint buds, small flowers, and the centers of flowers. These are just dots.

SPECIFIC PAINTING DIRECTIONS

Strawberries (Color picture, page 41)
1. Trace the design onto the fabric with pencil. The clusters in each corner of the label are the same, so you can trace both or either one twice.
2. Paint the strawberries as red ovals first. After they are dry, highlight with tiny dots of white and black.
3. Paint the leaves. Notice that the leaves are sketchy, not carefully outlined as strawberry leaves, but merely brush strokes, which begin at the fruit and fade at the outer edges. They merely *suggest* the leaf shapes, so you might not want to trace them too precisely on the first pencil sketch.

Pansies with Ribbon (Color picture, page 42)
1. Trace the drawing onto the fabric with pencil.
2. Paint the ribbon.
3. Paint the blue pansies.
4. Paint the leaves.
5. Shade and highlight the ribbon with white, the pansies with dark blue, the pansy centers with yellow dots and black lines.

Field of Flowers (Color picture, page 42)

1. Trace the drawing onto the fabric with pencil. Across the bottom, trace only the approximate outline of where you will want the edges of the grass to be.

2. Across the bottom, paint the leaves and grass, using the lightest green paint with sketchy brush strokes and leaving open white space. You can always fill in more later.

3. With a darker green, add some dark leaves, again sketchy suggestions.

4. Using red, add the flowers on top of the green. Add more or fewer than in the photograph; it doesn't matter. Notice, however, that most of these flowers are clustered at the two ends of the field.

5. Add spikey stalks going up from the field.

6. Along these stalks, add dots—some yellow and some blue.

7. Fill in with leaves as necessary.

8. On the side designs, paint over the traced outlines.

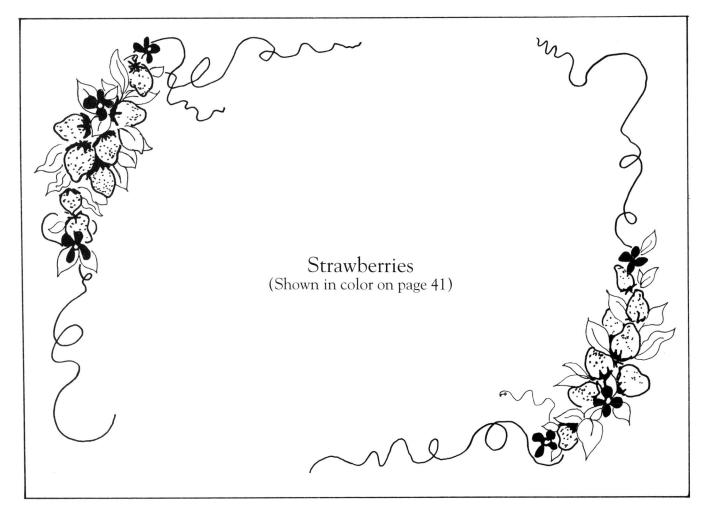

Strawberries
(Shown in color on page 41)

Pansies with Ribbon
(Shown in color on page 42)

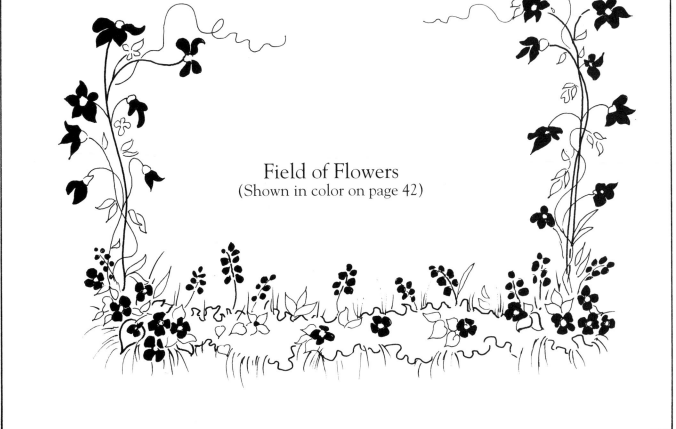

Field of Flowers
(Shown in color on page 42)

Chapter 15
Labels Painted With Fabric Dye
designed by Pauline Trout

With fabric markers and fabric dye pens, you can draw beautiful quilt labels, colorful yet quick and easy to make. Pauline Trout, a decorative painter turned quilter, uses fabric markers to embellish any fabric from clothing to quilts. Through her company, The Quail and Poppy, she designs charming quilt patterns that lend themselves equally well to appliqué and painting. When I saw her beautiful drawing on quilts, I asked her to contribute some of her techniques to our treasury. She has designed two labels as examples and inspiration for drawing on fabric. Her techniques are easy to learn and so effective that with a little practice we all can use them.

Drawing Supplies

fabric dye pens: Fashion Craft™ by Sakura
Pigma .01 pen: black for outlining
fabric: prewashed and ironed
extra fabric: for cushioning
an iron: to set dyes

FASHION CRAFT™ FABRIC MARKERS BY SAKURA

These pens are felt tip pens, which contain fabric dye and come in 24 colors from primary to pastel and even include some fluorescent colors. The felt tip provides good control with no bleeding and crayon-like color, either rich and clear or pale and sketchy, depending on how you hold the pen. The dye is permanent when heat set. The pens come conveniently packaged in two different sets of 12, either primary/basic colors or pastel/fluorescent colors. The directions for heat setting are on the package.

Angle of the Pen

The angle at which you hold the pen determines the style of line you get. Hold the pen upright as if you are writing, and you will get a precise line full of ink and, therefore, deep in color. Held on its side, the pen provides a pale, sketchy color.

Watercolor Effects

After coloring an element, you can turn it into a watercolor drawing by using cotton swabs dabbed in water. Within 20 minutes of coloring, dampen the swab and rub over the colors lightly. They will blend and soften, becoming a wash. You can still blend and shade, but the final effect is much softer than the original drawing. If the fabric gets too wet, iron it on the wrong side to dry it slightly. After "watercoloring," you can go over the colors again if they have faded too much.

GENERAL DIRECTIONS FOR DRAWING ON FABRIC WITH FASHION CRAFT PENS

1. Because you want the drawn flowers to have a carefree, sketchy look, do not trace the line drawings provided in the book onto your fabric. If you need an outline, make a marking guide on a piece of fabric. This outline need not be precise—it is just to show the general areas you will color.

2. Place the label fabric on several layers of fabric for cushioning, with the marking guide as the top layer of the cushion. The cushion changes the pen pressure and, thus, gives a softer look to the floral design.

3. There are three types of pen strokes: outline, sketch, and squiggle.

   a. Outline: Hold the pen upright and with light pressure, use the point to make a line. Use for outlines, vines, and scrolls. The line may be sketchy and broken.

   b. Sketch: Hold the pen on its side, and with a light touch, apply the color in a sweeping motion, turning the fabric as you fill in color.

   c. Squiggle: Hold the pen upright, and with light pressure, draw short, jagged, or curved lines. These suggest leaf and flower shapes.

DIRECTIONS FOR GERANIUMS OR ANY LARGE PETALS AND LEAVES

(Color picture, page 43)

1. Layer the fabric to cushion. Include a marking guide if you wish.
2. Use the point of the red pen to outline the petals.
3. Use the sketch stroke to apply color from the flower center out to each petal edge in curving lines. Shade at least one petal on both sides to prevent a pinwheel effect.

4. Lightly shade the outside edges of the petals, leaving the petal centers without color for highlights.
5. Go over the centers again, if necessary, to shade.
6. Leaves: Use the point of the green pen to outline the leaf. Carefully use the point to get close to the flower petals. Shade, putting the deepest color at the center of the leaf and next to the flower petals. Leave the outer leaf edges lighter for contrast.
7. Deepen the color of the leaves with a blue pen. Color again lightly with the green.
8. Outline the flowers and leaves with the Pigma .01 black pen. Use a light, carefree touch, not precise lines.

DIRECTIONS FOR PURPLE MUMS OR ANY THIN-PETALED FLOWER (Color picture, page 43)

1. These flowers are drawn with very free, light lines, using the outline stroke and drawing from the flower center out.
2. Shade the flower center and leave the outside points light.
3. The leaves are squiggles that overlap irregularly.
4. Outline with the Pigma .01 black pen and a sketchy, broken stroke.

Geraniums
(Shown in color on page 43)

Purple Mums
(Shown in color on page 43)

Chapter 16
Stenciled Labels

designed by Nancy Tribolet and Susan McKelvey

A stenciled label is an option worth considering. With stenciling, color is applied quickly and with spectacular results. So many stencils are available today in all sizes from miniature to full size that your choices are limited only by your imagination.

A search of quilt and craft supply stores will inspire you with the stenciling options. Two easy stencils are shown in this book—a wreath perfect for a small label and a border containing boughs of leaves. Each is done in several colors. Nancy Tribolet, a stencil designer and teacher from Houston, Texas, designed and painted Stenciled Boughs, and Susan McKelvey painted the Love Bird Wreath.

When considering stencils for your labels, keep in mind the design and layout considerations in Chapter 1. Just as you can stamp, appliqué, or trace any design or combination of designs in any location on a label, so, too, you can stencil anywhere. A pretty flower may go in a corner, with a leaf cluster opposite. Don't feel limited by the layout of the stencil as shown on its packaging or intimidated by its total size. If you like just one element in the stencil, you can use only that part on your label.

Stenciling Supplies

stencil
stencil brush: a flat, broad, stiff brush
acrylic paint, paint sticks, or **stencil paint creme**
newspaper or **paper towels**
masking tape

GENERAL STENCILING DIRECTIONS

1. Practice first on scrap pieces of the label fabric.

2. Work on a flat, smooth surface. You may want to work on a light box if you need to see placement marks.

3. Mark the fabric, if necessary; if you mark the outer borders, you can measure in from them. Or make a paper marking guide to place beneath the label.

4. Tape the fabric in place on the work surface or light box (over the marking guide if it's being used).

5. If there are sections of the stencil you are not using and they are near the section you will be working on, tape over them with masking tape. Leave a folded-under corner of the tape to act as a tab for easy removal.

6. Tape the stencil in place over the fabric.

7. The goal in stenciling is to brush on lightly for a soft look, then add paint if you want an opaque look.

   Liquid Paint: If you use liquid paint, the brush must be very dry. Dip only the end of the brush into the paint, then dab the brush repeatedly around a sheet of newspaper until almost all of the paint is absorbed and the brush is very dry.

   Stencil Paint Creme: Paint creme makes stenciling easy because it won't seep under the stencil. It is a concentrated paint that goes onto the fabric like rouge. Rub the brush on the paint creme; your brush is automatically dry.

8. For two-color, shaded stenciling, paint the light color first.

9. Use a light, circular brush stroke, working around each stencil hole from the plastic edge inward. Apply very little paint.

10. After the light color has dried, shade with a darker one. Again, stroke the brush from the outside edges inward, covering only a tiny bit of the previous color. Use the same procedure for shading any design element. Brown paint is a good choice for shading almost any color.

11. Remove the stencil, let it dry, and write the words on the label.

SPECIFIC STENCILING DIRECTIONS

Stenciled Boughs by Nancy Tribolet: (Color photograph on page 45) Nancy used two colors of Delta Stencil Paint Cremes, green and paprika, and a Stencil Magic stencil. She applied the green first, then added touches of the paprika. Detailing was added with the brown Pigma .01 pen.

Love Bird Wreath by Susan McKelvey: (Color photograph on page 45) Susan used two colors of liquid stencil paint and a Monogram Stencil by Plaid Enterprises. Detailing was added with a Pigma .01 pen and acrylic paint.

Chapter 17
Photo Transfers on Labels

designed by Susan McKelvey and custom made by Foto Fabrics

This exciting new technique provides us with a way to include actual photographs on our labels. You can transfer pictures onto fabric yourself with a variety of transfer techniques, but I have been delighted with the work of a company in Texas, Fabric Fotos, which has developed two useful processes. The first is a process for putting fabric directly through a copy machine for accurate one-color photo transfer and the second is a four-color heat transfer of photographs, which produces a photograph on fabric that is soft and pliable rather than thick and rubbery. The label shown on page 48 has been done combining the two techniques. The black borders were done on a copy machine; the color photographs are heat transfers. I designed the labels and sent the artwork, photographs, and directions to Fabric Fotos, and they produced this exquisite label. I then inked the documentation. Fabric Fotos will custom make a label for you from your artwork, or they have a selection of borders and phrases from which you may choose. They will also print the photographs you want on pieces of muslin so that you can sew them into your quilt in any way you choose. These photographs can be full color or one color.

Whether you experiment with photo-transferring onto fabric yourself or have the process done for you, the concept offers numerous creative opportunities for both labels and quilts. Look at *The Wedding Label* on page 48 for inspiration.

Chapter 18
Envelopes for Labels
designed by Susan McKelvey

An exciting addition to labels are fabric pockets or envelopes in which to tuck the labels or other precious quilt-related information. Some possible items to include:

scraps of fabric for repair   a photo of the maker or makers
a letter describing the quilt's history   a photo of the recipient
a photo of the quilt   extra buttons, thread, ribbons, etc.

This is an option filled with possibilities for extensive documentation of the quilt or for adding fun paraphernalia. It is, of course, not as secure as quilting the label into the quilt, but fun for the keepers of the flame of quilting to delve into or add to. In my quest for antique quilts, I have come across several with yellowed paper pinned or sewn to the back upon which was written, in the shaky hand of elderly relatives, some sketchy information on the quilts' histories. How excited and grateful I would be if I came across an old quilt in a trunk with an envelope on the back filled with a yellowed note actually provided by the maker containing information on that specific quilt. That would be a treasure indeed. Just in case you want to add such a treasure to accompany your quilt on its journey into history, I have provided the patterns for fabric envelopes in which to tuck your "historical treasures."

I have been playing with envelopes on both the fronts and backs of my quilts, and have enjoyed the freedom they allow me. If you, too, are intrigued by the possibilities of envelopes on quilts, try any one of the three pattern sizes for envelopes and the letters to go inside them provided here. You may adapt any decorative techniques or any label designs to these. Also, consider other wonderful possibilities for using fabric envelopes. Make an envelope into a soft card, a jewelry case, a pillow front, a love token or Valentine, a sewing case or a gift package. See pages 46 and 47 for color pictures of envelopes.

ENVELOPE DIRECTIONS

> ### Supplies
> **fabric:** any you prefer, 9" x 12" for the smallest evelope, 12" x 14" for the middle size, and 13" x 17" for the largest
> **notions:** tiny snaps, decorative buttons or rosettes, ribbon
> **permanent pen**
> **sewing equipment**
> **optional:** thin batting, enough for the label/letter

1. Cut two pieces of the chosen envelope, one in fabric to match or complement the quilt backing, one for the envelope lining in muslin (if you want to draw on it) or a complementary fabric. The patterns are given without seam allowances, so be sure to add either $1/4$" (to trim to $1/8$" after sewing) or $1/8$".
2. Draw on the muslin piece before sewing, following "Drawing Directions" on the next page.
3. Lay the two envelope pieces right sides together. Pin. Sew all around, turning sharply at inside points and leaving open between hearts for turning.
4. Trim to $1/8$". Turn right side out, working out the corners. Press. Whip the opening closed.
5. Fold along the folding guide lines. Press.

6. Hand sew the envelope together with matching thread. Fold in the two side flaps first. They overlap. Tack them together. Cover them with the bottom flap, and sew along its edges.

7. Attach the snap to appropriate spot on top and bottom flaps.

8. Add a decorative button or ribbon.

9. To quilt or not? Since this envelope is going onto a quilt that is already thick, it should be as thin as possible. Therefore, if you want to quilt it, don't use any batting. However, it will look fine unquilted. The samples are unquilted.

10. Attach the envelope to the quilt with a blind stitch.

SEWING DIRECTIONS FOR LABELS OR LETTERS

1. Cut two from the label pattern—either both in muslin or the back in a contrasting fabric. The label patterns are given without seam allowances, so add either $1/8$" or $1/4$".

2. Decorate and write on the muslin label/letter, one side or both, following the "Drawing Directions" below.

3. Lay the two pieces right sides together. Pin. If you are using batting in the middle, layer like this: batting, label front and label back, right sides facing. Sew all around, leaving open between the hearts for turning.

4. Trim to $1/8$". Turn right side out. Press.

5. Hand sew the opening closed.

6. Insert it into the envelope. Leave it loose or, to be sure it doesn't get lost, attach it to one corner of the envelope with a ribbon leash. Decorate the ribbon with a button or bow.

7. If you inserted batting, you might want to quilt the label a little. The sample labels have no batting and are not quilted.

DRAWING DIRECTIONS

I have included some traceable designs to use on the envelopes and letters. In addition, use any designs scattered throughout the book that might be appropriate.

Envelopes

Decide whether to decorate the inside or the outside. If the inside, there is only one place that shows—the upper border. Choose a border and draw it about $1/2$" from the seamline. Remember to account for the seam allowance. If you choose to decorate the outside, you have more options—corners or border or both.

Labels

Make a border either part way or all the way around the label. Use a bow or basket in one corner or two. Mix the bows and borders.

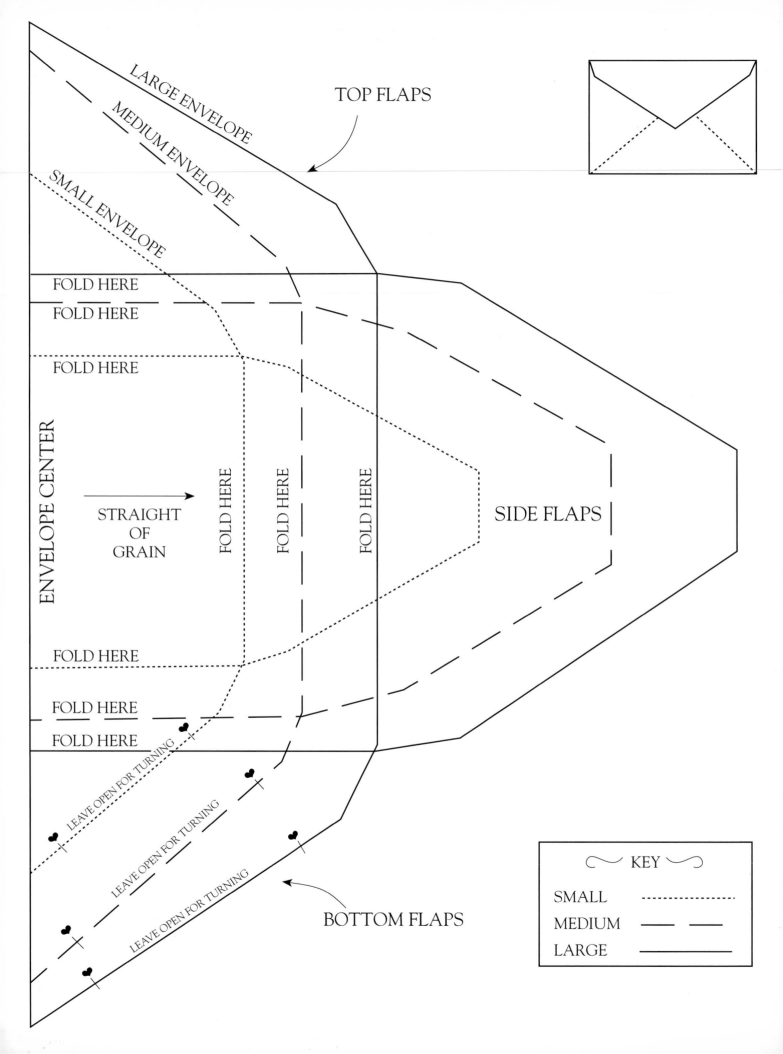

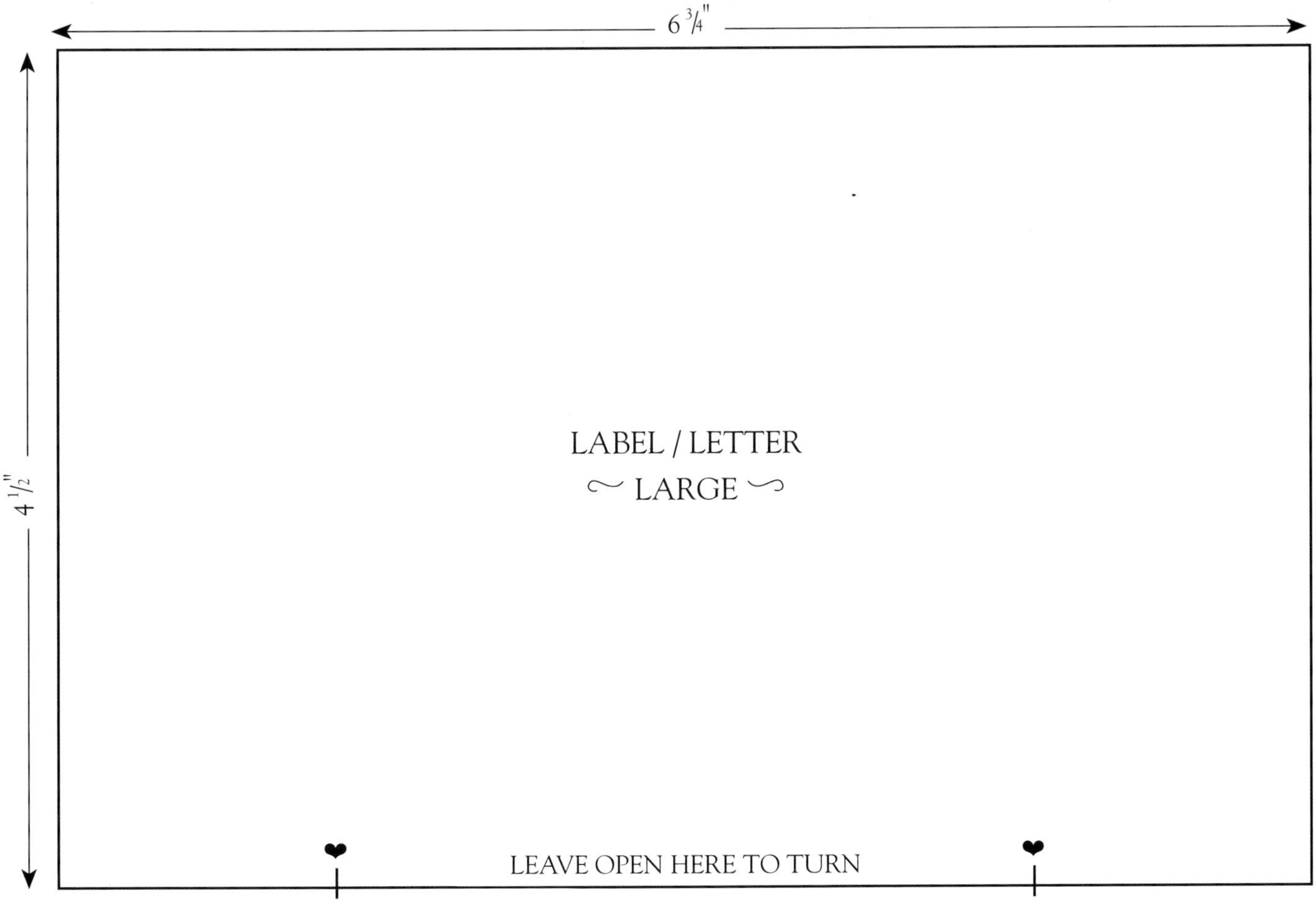

6 ¾"

LABEL / LETTER
～ LARGE ～

4 ½"

LEAVE OPEN HERE TO TURN

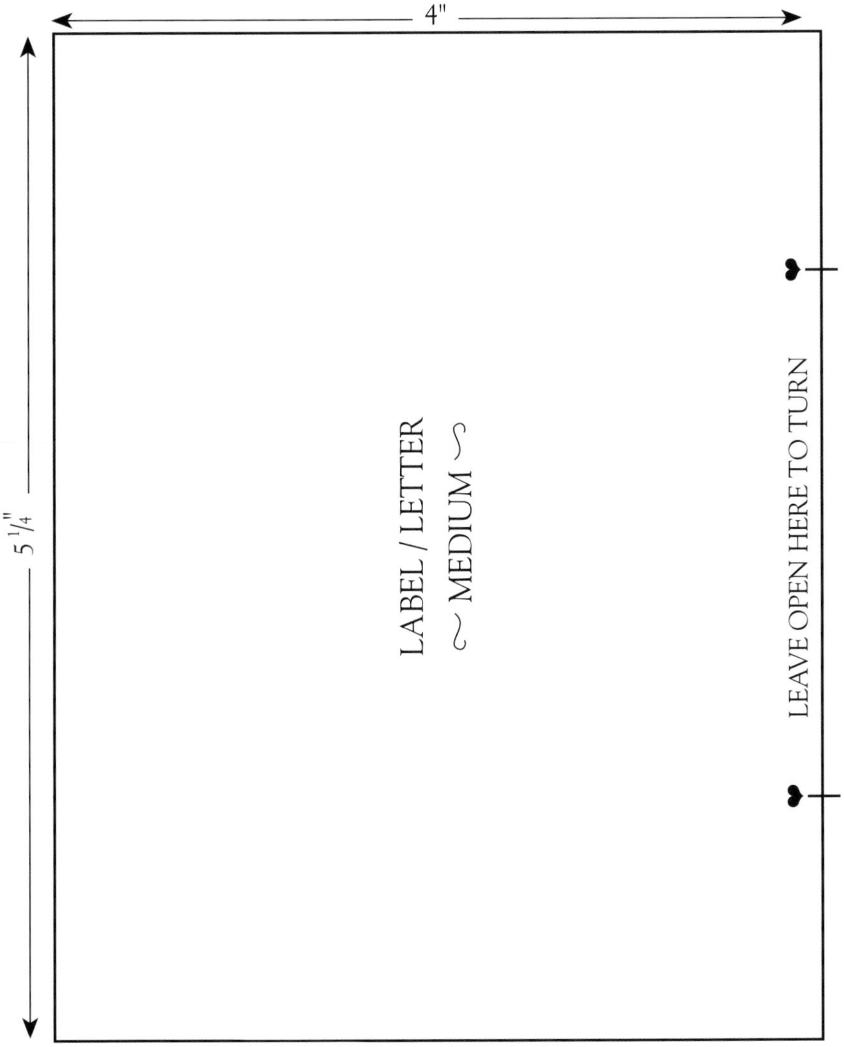

4"

LABEL / LETTER
～ MEDIUM ～

5 ¼"

LEAVE OPEN HERE TO TURN

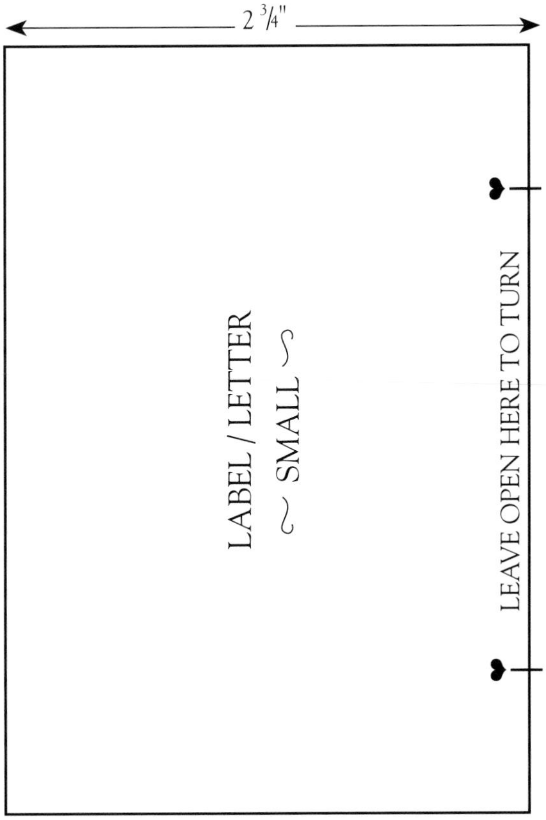

2 ¾"

4"

LABEL / LETTER
～ SMALL ～

LEAVE OPEN HERE TO TURN

Part Four

Tying Up
Loose
Ends

Susan Sbonesi

The Designers

Pele Fleming is a quilter who lives in the mountains north of Santa Cruz, California, with her husband, two daughters, two horses, and two parakeets. She is the owner of Pelle's, a family company that manufactures stamps and related supplies for stamping on textiles.

Sandy Flores lives in Sebastopol, California, with her husband and two children. Until she discovered Brazilian embroidery twelve years ago, she enjoyed a variety of needlearts, but she now specializes in Brazilian techniques, teaching and selling the supplies through her business, Sandy's Fancy Threads.

Jackie Janovsky is a quilt artist who lives in Annapolis, Maryland, with her husband and two college-aged daughters. She spends as much time as possible quilting, and teaches quilting and needlearts such as smocking and French hand sewing through Adult Education classes. Her great love in quilting is hand appliqué.

Anna Macaluso lives in Totowa, New Jersey, and she is an artist with interests in many crafts from woodcarving to quilting—with quilting at the top of the list. Born in Bologna, Italy, she came to the United States in 1971. She has been designing and painting quilt labels for herself and friends for several years.

Rhoda Miller resides in Annapolis, Maryland, with her husband and two grown daughters. Prior to her introduction to quilting twelve years ago she had done many kinds of needlework, but her current loves are quilting and making bears and dolls.

Dawnell Reeves was born and raised in the Pacific Northwest where she currently resides with her husband and two daughters. For the last decade, she has run the largest craft boutique in her area. In 1991, after being introduced to hand appliqué, she and her friend Carol Shoaf started a pattern company called Legacy in Stitches, which sells Dawnell's designs and Carol's hand-dyed fabric.

Nancy Tribolet is a stenciler and decorative painter who resides in Houston, Texas, where she teaches stenciling and has designed her own line of stencils, including a group of stencils for Delta.

Pauline Trout has been quilting since 1974 and founded her business, The Quail and Poppy, in 1980 to sell decorative painting supplies. In 1985 she moved to Southern California and began showing her quilts, which won awards and inspired her to design appliqué quilt patterns. She currently designs and sells the patterns through The Quail and Poppy.

Sources

Appliqué Patterns

Legacy in Stitches, 720 N. Green, Kennewick, WA 99336, (509) 783-7804, Dawnell Reeves and
        Carol Shoaf.
The Quail and Poppy, 1189 West Evergreen St., Rialto, CA 92376, (714) 820-1250, Pauline Trout.
Wallflower Designs, 1161 Goldfinch Lane, Millersville, MD 21108, (410) 923-6895, Susan McKelvey.

Books

C & T Publishing, P.O. Box 1456, Lafayette, CA 94549, (510) 370-9600, (800) 284-1114.

Brazilian Embroidery Supplies

Sandy's Fancy Threads, 1312 Jonive Rd., Sebastopol, CA 94572, (707) 823-6624, Sandy Flores.

Custom Photo Transfer

Fabric Fotos, 3801 Olsen Blvd. #3, Amarillo, TX 79109, (806) 359-8241.

Hand-Dyed and Hand-Marbeled Fabrics

Legacy in Stitches, 720 N. Green, Kennewick, WA 99336, (509) 783-7804, Dawnell Reeves and
        Carol Shoaf.
Shades Inc. 2880 Holcomb Bridge Road, #B-9, Alpharetta, GA 30202, (800) 783-3933, Stacy Michell.

Labels

Wallflower Designs, 1161 Goldfinch Lane, Millersville, MD 21108, (410) 923-6895, Susan McKelvey.

Light Boxes

Me Sew Co., 24307 Magic Mountain Pkwy., Suite 195, Valencia, CA, 91355, (800) 846-3739,
        Margie Evans.

Stamping Supplies

Pelle's, P.O. Box 242, Davenport, CA 95017, (408) 425-4743, Pele Fleming.

Stenciling Supplies

Delta Technical Coatings, Inc., 2550 Pellesier Place, Whittier, CA 90601-1505, (800) 423-4135.
Plaid Enterprises, 1649 International Blvd., Norcross, GA 30091-7600.
Stencil Designs by Nancy, 15206 Walters Rd., Houston, TX 77068, (713) 893-6187, Nancy Tribolet.

Writing Supplies: Pens and Traceable Designs

Wallflower Designs, 1161 Goldfinch Lane, Millersville, MD 21108, (410) 923-6895, Susan McKelvey.

Bibliography

Bernath, Stefen. *Floral Spot Illustrations*. Dover Publications, Mineola, NY, 1989.

Croner, Marjorie. *Fabric Photos*. Interweave Press, Loveland, CO, 1989.

McKelvey, Susan. *Friendship's Offering*. C & T Publishing, Lafayette, CA, 1987.

_____. *Scrolls & Banners to Trace*. Wallflower Designs, Millersville, MD, 1990.

_____. *More Scrolls & Banners*. Wallflower Designs, Millersville, MD, 1991.

Menton, Ted. *Ready-to-Use Decorative Corners*. Dover Publications, Mineola, NY, 1987.

Ritter, Vivian Howell. *Family Keepsake Quilts*. Leman Publications, Inc., Wheat Ridge, CO, 1991.

Sienkiewicz. Elly. *Baltimore Beauties and Beyond*. C & T Publishing, Lafayette, CA, 1989.

Sully, Primrose. *Stunning Stitches*. Primrose Sully, New South Wales, Australia, 1990.

Takahashi, Kiyoshi. *Ready-to-Use Calligraphic Ornaments*. Dover Publications, Mineola, NY, 1983.

_____. *Calligraphic Ornaments & Borders*. Graphic Products Corporation, Wheeling, IL, 1989.

OTHER FINE QUILTING BOOKS FROM C & T PUBLISHING

Appliqué 12 Easy Ways!, Elly Sienkiewicz
The Art of Silk Ribbon Embroidery, Judith Montano
Baltimore Beauties and Beyond (2 Volumes), Elly Sienkiewicz
Christmas Traditions From the Heart, Margaret Peters
Crazy Quilt Handbook, Judith Montano
Heirloom Machine Quilting, Harriet Hargrave
Imagery on Fabric, Jean Ray Laury
Isometric Perspective, Katie Pasquini-Masopust
The Magical Effects of Color, Joen Wolfrom
Mastering Machine Appliqué, Harriet Hargrave
Memorabilia Quilting, Jean Wells
Recollections, Judith Montano
Whimsical Animals, Miriam Gourley

For more information write for a free catalog from
C & T Publishing
P.O. Box 1456
Lafayette, CA 94549

About the Author

Susan McKelvey is a quilt artist, teacher, and the author of several books on quilting besides *A Treasury of Quilt Labels*. Those titles include *Color for Quilters*, *The Color Workbook*, *Light & Shadows*, *Friendship's Offering*, *Scrolls & Banners to Trace*, and *More Scrolls and Banners*. Her great love in quilting is color and helping quilters to use color effectively in their work.

Susan has been quilting since 1977, and her work has appeared in museums, galleries, and quilt shows throughout the United States, as well as in magazines and books. She began her own company, Wallflower Designs, in 1987 to design and produce supplies and patterns for quilters who want to write on quilts.

In the days before quilting, Susan earned her B.A. degree in English and Drama at Cornell College and her M.A. in English and Education at the University of Chicago.

A Treasury of Quilt Labels grew out of Susan's interest in writing on quilts and was inspired by the creativity of the quilters she has met through her traveling and teaching.